PRAISE F

THE EXTRAVAGANT FOOL

With gentleness and personal vulnerability, Kevin Adams takes us on his compelling journey and challenges us to "waste our life for God." His example, during horrific circumstances, of a person walking by faith and totally reliant on God is a remarkable testimony to God's faithfulness. Kevin shows us all how we can set aside our own foolish thoughts and be all-out, radical fools for God.

Wayne Hastings, resources pastor at Grace Chapel, Leipers Fork, Tennessee, and author of *The Way Back from Loss*

In *The Extravagant Fool*, Kevin Adams brilliantly uses his gift of storytelling to put everyday life in the context of God's plan. You'll discover how God does both the simple and the extraordinary to get our attention, shake up our faith, and align our story with His. Brimming with real life and wisdom, this book is evidence that our extravagant God is truly our greatest reward.

Tami Heim, president and CEO of Christian Leadership Alliance

Kevin Adams pens the details of his journey to authentic faith with stunning beauty and brutal honesty. *The Extravagant Fool* brings our truest purpose in life into clearest focus—love God above all else. Only in this place of childlike faith do we find peace, rest, and hope.

Dineen Miller, coauthor of *Winning Him without Words* and *Not Alone* and author of *The Soul Saver*

Devastatingly powerful! Can faith carry you through a season of temporary suffering? Kevin's evocative writing and introspection compel you to lean in and discover that God is abundantly more than we hope, more than we believe, and always more than we can see.

Lynn Donovan, coauthor of *Winning Him
without Words* and *Not Alone*

If you're having trouble striking a balance between sermons of Utopian Christian promise and the difficulty of daily life, read this book! Kevin Adams takes us on a thrill ride of hope that will give the most desperately struggling believer increasing faith for God's best.

Bill Spencer, executive director of Narrow Gate Foundation

With nakedly honest reflection, Kevin Adams has penned a book I've always wanted to read but hadn't found anyone vulnerable enough to write. *The Extravagant Fool* takes us through his "perfect storm" to a place of hope, healing, and authentic restoration.

Gari Meacham, popular speaker and author
of *Watershed Moments*, *Spirit Hunger*, and *Truly Fed*

Kevin's perfect storm reveals the painful reality of fear and unmitigated loss. He poignantly talks about issues much of the church will not touch—like questioning God and wondering if He really does see us, know us, or is moved by our plight. Kevin refuses to candy-coat his dark night of the soul but continues to bring us back to a hope that will not let go—to a Savior who still calms the sea of our heart. This is the best book I've read in a long time. It is riveting from start to finish! Are you struggling with loss and disappointment, feel like you're swimming in the mud of disillusionment in God's ways? This book is for you!

Tammy Maltby, speaker and author of *The God Who Sees You*

In a world that has turned the meaning of true wisdom and riches on its head, we need an extravagant fool to help us off the hamster wheel of "do more, strive more, spend more." This disruptive book reveals how being a "good Christian" isn't the same as radically following Christ. It's the riveting story of a man who had it all, lost it all, had the chance to regain worldly success, walked away, and at great cost found the true gold we all long for. But be warned — reading this story may be God's invitation to rewrite your own story in the most extravagantly foolish way imaginable. Are you ready?

Allen Arnold, director of content and resources at Ransomed Heart Ministries

In *The Extravagant Fool*, I was reminded of Jim Elliot's words, "He is no fool who gives what he cannot keep to gain that which he cannot lose." This is the lesson Kevin Adams learned — and lived. May his journey encourage your faith.

Laurie Short, author of *Finding Faith in the Dark*

Kevin Adams is a modern-day hero of the faith. In *The Extravagant Fool*, Kevin candidly unveils his life and how uncompromising faith can be awakened amid tremendous loss, grief, and betrayal. If status quo faith isn't enough for you — get this book!

Joy Scott, founder of Joseph's Joy Foundation

Kevin Adams is a powerful writer whose authenticity and gritty faith will keep you riveted with every page turn. Few writers are willing to be as transparent, and you will cry and celebrate with him as if his life were your own. *The Extravagant Fool* is a roller-coaster ride of inspiration and challenges. Thank you, Kevin, for sharing your life in a way that touched my own. I truly love this book!

Lyn Smith, speaker and collaborative writer with Tommy Newberry of *Think 4:8*

Authentic, poignant, and excellently written, *The Extravagant Fool* is rich with wise and timely words for this generation. This book will help you write a better story with the pages of your life.

Michael Neale, national bestselling author
of *The River* and Dove Award-winning songwriter

Kevin Adams is an unflinching guide into largely unexplored territory — the up-side of upside-down kingdom living. Follow this "extravagant fool" to the place where faith and need collide, producing a life marked by the surprising activity of God. Read this beautiful work of grace, and come out changed.

Allison Allen, speaker, author, and actor whose credits
include Broadway, Women of Faith, and *Magdalene*

THE EXTRAVAGANT FOOL

KEVIN ADAMS

THE
EXTRAVAGANT FOOL

A FAITH JOURNEY THAT BEGINS
WHERE COMMON SENSE ENDS

ZONDERVAN

The Extravagant Fool
Copyright © 2014 by Kevin Adams

This title is also available as a Zondervan ebook. Visit www.zondervan.com/ebooks.

Requests for information should be addressed to:

Zondervan, 3900 *Sparks Drive SE, Grand Rapids, Michigan 49546*

Library of Congress Cataloging-in-Publication Data

Adams, Kevin, 1966-
        The extravagant fool : a faith journey that begins where common sense ends /
Kevin Adams.
            p. cm.
        ISBN 978-0-310-33796-6 (hardcover)
        1. Adams, Kevin, 1966-. 2. Christian biography—United States. I. Title.
BR1725.A293A3 2014
277.3'083092—dc23   2013044786

The author is represented by the literary agency of Alive Communications, Inc., 7680 God-
dard Street, Suite 200, Colorado Springs, CO 80920, www.alivecommunications.com.

Cover design: Curt Diepenhorst
Cover photography: Getty Images®
Interior design and illustrations: David Conn

Printed in the United States of America

Thank You, Father, for teaching me to rest in Your arms like a happy child, and to write this by faith when doing so appeared to be the whim of a fool. This book belongs to You. May it be well received as living proof of Your boundless love and generosity toward Your children, and may it leave a lasting impression on all who decide to read it that You really are that good — always better than any of us can imagine.

CONTENTS

PART 1: BECOMING A FOOL ...
THE IRRATIONAL CALL OF GOD

1 THROWN IN THE WELL..15
2 DRIVEN 29
3 OKAY, GOD ... IT'S YOUR MOVE 41
4 IF THERE'S ANYTHING WE CAN DO 57

PART 2: CONFOUNDING THE WISE

5 EMBRACING THE MYSTERY 69
6 THE HOMELESS LANDLORD...77
7 NOT "THE PROVIDER"...85
8 THE "KNOCKOFF"...95
9 SURRENDER 107
10 FAITH PENDULUM 129

PART 3: THE GAMBLE

11 REST 145
12 WAKE UP MY FAITH 153
13 JUST ENOUGH SAND 167
14 OKAY, LIFE'S UNFAIR ... WHERE DO WE GO
   FROM HERE? 179

PART 4: A FOOL'S REWARD ...
AN EXTRAVAGANT GOD

15 MASHED POTATO 197
16 ONLY WHEN GOD BECOMES ALL THAT WE WANT........205

ACKNOWLEDGMENTS...219

PART 1

BECOMING A FOOL...
THE IRRATIONAL CALL
OF GOD

CHAPTER 1

THROWN IN THE WELL

The fall season has arrived as an empty-handed messenger. The income we'd hoped to see remains the income we hope to see eventually. Until then, we've stopped paying our mortgage in order to cover essentials. Better to face foreclosure in the next few months than to face the next few weeks without food and utilities. With little memory of God's sweetness there is nothing to do but wait, and wonder aloud if He is still generous. All I have is failure to cover my need, and not a clue what a generous God might do with such an extravagant fool.

Faith Journal, November 2011

THE VIEW FROM ABOVE — OCTOBER 2008

There was something hypnotic about swiveling my chair back and forth between the windows. The backside of our house overlooked a valley dotted with overweight custom homes, and people on golf carts threading between them while talking on their phones. But not everything that rhymes is poetic, and some things are only beautiful when we squint. Just a half block up in front, on the neighborhood's highest peak, stood the largest home for miles at about fourteen thousand square feet, pushing its way through my office window like ambition pushes its way through a man's character. In a community full of ambitious people with clean fingernails and perfectly trimmed lawns, a generation of sprinters lined up for a race that for most is actually a marathon.

It was the fall of 2008 when the phone finally rang, and my largest client hadn't paid us for months. On my desk sat stacks of receivables — hundreds of unpaid bills owed by hundreds of companywide buyers, people always in a jam. I spun my chair away from the window and back again, wondering if I should answer.

"Mr. Adams, this is the finance department, and I'm the new CFO. It appears we have a backlog of unpaid invoices from your company. Do you have a few minutes to discuss?"

"Certainly," I said.

"Sorry for the inconvenience," he said, "but we've been working on the budget and don't quite have a handle on what your company does for us."

I paused, considering why a client I'd been serving for years was asking what we do for them. Translation: *We're making sure we no longer need what your company does for us.* Another thirty seconds passed between the echo of throats being cleared and speakerphone whispers. "Actually, Mr. Adams, if you could just provide some detail on these invoices, we can begin working toward a settlement." Further translation: *Thanks, Mr. Adams ... it's been real!*

And it got even more real, as the phone began to ring with one call after another, asking the same emotionless question—"Why are we paying you?" Somehow I'd become a foreigner to anyone with an accounting degree. It was as if by UFO the CFOs had been flown in to save the world from everything nonessential. And by extension, my three large homes, my business condo, my company's value, and every penny of my income were now equally nonessential.

Where would this end up? I crossed my legs and slumped into my chair, causing it to drift slightly from the window. I suppose its hypnotic swivel had finally made me sick, homesick that is, for something more stable.

Our largest client withheld payment for so long before cutting ties that any final relief was instantly absorbed by creditors. All our clients in one form or another took the same posture—preserve thyself and ask questions later. With monthly expenses in the tens of thousands and suddenly no income, the ground does more than shake. My wife, Holly, and I have described it as a three-month earthquake that led to a four-year tsunami. But out of respect for victims of such tragic events, perhaps the term "perfect storm" is more appropriate.

A perfect storm is a rare combination of events whose effects are compounded exponentially when they intersect. I'd always heard that success is where hard work and opportunity intersect. I suppose without wisdom they amount to the same thing, because chasing success at any cost is like chasing that storm until it eventually reverses course—unless, of course, you are wise enough in advance to prepare a place to retreat. With several investment properties—an office condo and two large homes, not including our residence—the option to sell or borrow on equity was my retreat. Or so I thought.

When we started investing, home equity was rising by leaps and bounds, but the rental market was highly competitive.

Keeping our rental rates low ensured that the properties would remain occupied until we were ready to sell. Obviously, there's little wisdom in taking on tenants for the sole purpose of breaking even. But in a time when you can buy a house, paint the bonus room, and sell it for a fifty thousand dollar profit, subpar rental rates are a negligible trade for such a glorious upside. Also, our disposable income was high enough to avoid renters altogether, so the rates didn't seem to matter as much in the moment—a moment destined to intersect with my character.

A collapsing real estate market, along with the near collapse of our economy, set the stage. But it was my ambition and lack of wisdom that left us unprepared and ultimately stole the show—a show that went on for the next four years—a perfect storm of sorts.

In most financial downturns the dominoes fall one by one. Though painful to watch, there is time to consider the damage. Bad investments become lessons learned, and lost incomes are replaced. With hard work, those fallen pieces can be reset, but standing dominoes have less resistance in the wind of a perfect storm. With a company pulled out from under us and the simultaneous real estate implosion, our little wooden blocks were utterly blown off the table. Investments became debts, and debts without income became lawsuits.

There were simply no pieces left to set back up.

DESPAIR IN SLOW MOTION

With no pieces to pick up, no bootstraps to grab, there appeared to be no remedy—no possible escape through hard work. Our tenants were not sympathetic, and neither were most people who knew us, because nothing had changed in our immediate surroundings. Life is not a beach, but it must have appeared to some that we were carelessly basking on one.

Only my wife and I could see the approaching tidal wave. Hand in hand with our children playing behind us, completely unaware of its danger, we couldn't bring ourselves to turn around and explain it to them or anyone else. So we just stood there, not even looking at one another, waiting for impact while they laughed and argued with no appreciation of how good they'd had it. Like most of us.

It was one of those treacherous moments that occur in slow motion, but not so slow that one can escape it. So with both feet sinking into wet sand, I was forced to watch it helplessly while the unflinching world around me continued on, smiling. Golf carts still circled the block. Mothers talked on phones while buying groceries. No one knew, and God didn't seem to care.

I was angry with myself for what I had done to my family, and angry about what they would suffer. It would mean losing material wealth—past, present, and future—my career, our life savings, every investment, a company built from scratch, our home and nearly all that filled it, and every scrap of credit. And certainly it meant losing the freedom that those things provide, little things like piano lessons and haircuts, gas for the car and oil for the mower, shoes for the girls, and a microwave oven that works. But it would ultimately mean suffering through despair that no one around us could truly feel.

We'd been given a food basket that included a bag of microwave popcorn. Only the clock still worked on our oven, so we politely asked a neighbor to microwave it for us. Her response was an easygoing but slightly uncertain yes, followed by a pinch of passive sarcasm.

"You know, microwave ovens are not that expensive these days." My wife just smiled and kindly thanked her.

Private despair is also facing an empty cupboard while an armed messenger from the sheriff's department bangs at the door. It is wondering how long the electricity will stay on while pausing to consider if lights are more important than health insurance. And it is continuing on while new debts invisible to friends are being accrued from past mistakes—mistakes now inching us closer and closer to homelessness. But it's not about bootstraps or going back to zero and picking up the pieces, despite the well-intentioned sentiment of others.

JOB'S FRIENDS AND OURS

God is never silent by accident, but that doesn't stop us from making suggestions in His place to those with an unclear struggle. "Just turn your lemons into lemonade," we might say. Or how about this one: "If there's anything I can do"—said just before glancing at our watch and moving on. Whether our response originates from compassion or a stealthy means of escape, we all feel compelled to speak on occasion when God is silent. And for the hurting, the road to their hell-on-earth is, on occasion, paved with good intentions that we call words of wisdom.

While the neighborly make passing suggestions about lemons, others make standing proclamations, speaking not only in God's silence but apparently speaking on His behalf. I call these folks "Job's friends," and from the spiritual woodwork they come, marching in lockstep with their "keep your chin up and pray with your feet moving" regalia and the "it's all right, we've all been there" speech. For us they came ready to raise a spiritual barn, assuming our commitment to God needed an overhaul or a rebuilding with new timber.

"Looks like it's time to simplify your life — to cancel cable TV and cell phones, to stop eating out and buying junk food, and to live in a modest home. It's time to get off the floor and rebuild your company, or work several jobs, if necessary; time for the wife to get an income and make sure you are tithing as a family. It's time for you to humble yourself and cautiously remember that a man who works is one who eats and pays back every penny he owes. So if you'll roll up your sleeves and really commit, you'll find that God is waiting in the wings to help you. He always helps those who help themselves, and we always reap what we sow. We're praying for you."

Maybe they were right, but never before did something so practical seem so meaningless. I'd been a Christian all my life, and a committed one since I was eighteen. I knew there was more to this life than getting ourselves to the next one. But suddenly, at age forty, after years of commitment, I couldn't explain what "more to this life" actually meant. Were they saying that God would really leave us in the street to teach us deeper commitment? No one, of course, would say such a thing, but to a man in my position, that was the bottom line.

I once told someone emphatically that God would never allow that to happen. "Hopefully not," the man replied, "but if He does, you need to be prepared." How exactly does one prepare for that? In the heavenly silence the noisy world got noisier and the voices of those around me grew louder, until my wife, the voice that mattered more, was asking the same question of me that I was asking of God. *What are you doing?*

THE DO-IT-YOURSELF CHURCH

So for a time, I stopped asking God and looked to those around me, considering perhaps that God was speaking through others—others I hadn't considered, such as the church. Maybe they could fathom that when we said "complicated," we meant millions in debt, and when we said "everything," we meant there are no groceries. But their answers were the same proverbial, consider-the-ants practicality, and it would require more than canceling the cable and more than working an extra job to get us out of *this* mess. And ultimately it would take more wisdom than I possessed to explain something so far-reaching to those hard-working ants.

Yes, we tithed, gave generously, and served as faithful believers doing all the right things—none of which made any difference. But all the common-sense answers were pointing in the same direction. Every answer, every solution, was indistinguishable from the next—do more, prepare more, become this, give that, be more committed. *Do, do, do*—I was exhausted.

But with every passing hour their evidence mounted against us. We'd soon be forced from our home with no income, no credit, and three expensive properties that could no longer be supported or quickly sold. Finding a place to rent under these conditions was nearly impossible, and without a place to rent or family close by, there would be no place to catch our breath and nowhere to go after that—a certain death sentence.

Whether the judgment was aimed at rehabilitating our commitment or something more tenuous, the most painful thing was thinking that God had abandoned us—not our souls, but our welfare. I wasn't angry with God, only with where my understanding of the Christian life had led us—bad decisions based on things He expected of me, like providing, leading, and loving my family.

Ultimately, there would be no escape through doing more of the same, but even a glimpse of freedom through the ideas of other Christians would keep me trying until every high place from which to jump, every embankment, and every bottle of pills gave me pause. Death wasn't a relief for me as much as an offering to relieve my family *of* me—a last bold move that would provide them justice for my drive to succeed, mislead, and gamble with their lives. I pleaded for God to take my life, but something in His silence would not allow their relief to come through my absence.

Okay, God … it's Your move. People say they're afraid to ask God to do whatever it takes, or pray the "I'll do anything" prayer. But we were asking a different question, praying a different prayer—"God, there is nothing left for us to do—*now what?*" Résumés and rental inquiries flew from the keyboard and printer, but nothing returned—no olive branches or answers from God, and no calls from potential employers.

I sat in my car regularly for weeks to escape the absurdity of home—a new home worth only half its purchase price. Behind every open door lingered the aromas of oak floor, fresh paint, and new carpet. We'd only lived there a year. My faith reclined behind the wheel of the driver's seat as people rushed in and out of Target with expensive coffee and small children. *Where did they live?* I wondered, as I considered how a family of five might sleep, there on my fully reclined seats. There were different parking lots and different passersby, but no escape for me, as absurdity, it seemed, was a moving cloud with my name on it.

With kids as healthy as sunshine, a devoted wife, and no boils to scrape, my suffering was inconsequential next to Job's.

But I couldn't help wondering how he would handle such a mess as mine. I never doubted that God loved me, but I also believed that His love and care were based on my behavior. Oh, it's easy to say the opposite, but deep down there are few of us who don't trip over our own foibles and consider the pain of fixing-it-oneself to be a kind of "holy" responsibility.

TWO KINDS OF FOOLS

At one point, after studying the Bible for several hours, I began to feel a sense of encouragement that God was revealing something about my own "holy" responsibility, and I was eventually drawn to this verse.

> Do not deceive yourselves. If any of you think you are wise by the standards of this age, you should become "fools" so that you may become wise.
>
> 1 Corinthians 3:18

Through this verse God revealed to me that there are essentially two kinds of fools—one who says (or lives as if) there is no God, and one who lives as if there's nothing worthwhile outside of God. Which is a clear-cut distinction that forces us to choose between the two, immediately. Until that moment, I had always believed I was the right kind of fool, but after further meditation, I began to see things a little more clearly.

For instance, becoming a genuine fool for God is as simple for many believers as taking the moral high ground by remaining humble in an argument, or avoiding worldly practices such as dishonesty, greed, selfishness, and the like. While at the same time, we engage in less obvious practices, such as leaning on our own understanding, applying moderation to our faith in

God, making our decisions by the spirit of fear and calling it wisdom, or even placing the desires of our spouses or children above God—and the list goes on.

So as far as I could discern, especially through the eyes of our circumstances, merely avoiding the obvious and calling it godly foolishness wasn't enough. But becoming a *genuine* fool for God, and gaining true wisdom from His Spirit, required the willingness to let go of one's own understanding and go against the tide of popular ideas that seem sensible on the surface, but underneath remain inadvertently swayed by things outside of God. It was at this critical moment in my life when I could finally see that the bottom line was about making the right choice—deciding which type of fool to become, and either wasting my life for God or simply wasting it.

BY GEORGE—I THINK THE FOOL HAS IT

Therefore, I asked God for the faith to become the right kind of fool—an extravagant one! But what He gave me instead was an example of one with a flawed character like my own, who wasn't on a scriptural pedestal—a modern example, this side of King James—who by faith became a fool for God, just as any hero of Scripture had done.

I suppose the reason for this was that as a modern Christian, like most, I couldn't see the incredibly subtle differences between what I claimed as truth and how I responded when the facts opposed it. In other words, when our absolute faith in Scripture goes unchecked, practicality takes over by subconsciously rationalizing biblical heroics as "God's sovereignty," and our own daily events as "concrete reality." And we end up with an absolutely mechanical faith—one that operates on the one-way parts of logic. As a result, we then continue on with our "standards of this age" way of life, and never know the difference.

So God opened my eyes in a way that I could accept while I was still very immature in my faith. And he did so by giving me an example of what being a fool looked like, and a testimony of what living by faith could do, to reconnect me with the truth that "reality" *is* what we find in Scripture. The testimony I'm referring to is that of George Müller. Ironically, I had read his autobiography a decade before and been so frightened by it that I never wanted to see it again. But there it was on my bookshelf, untouched for a decade, and there I was with nothing left to lose.

George Müller was an ordinary man who, after a life of rebellion, surrendered his heart to the Lord and became a preacher of the gospel during the mid-nineteenth century. He later heard the call of God to establish a house for the care and education of orphans in Bristol, England. He answered that call without any means of support, fully expecting that God alone would move the hearts of men to meet every need.

With childlike faith he looked only to God through prayerful petition and found that every need was punctually met for decades. Over the course of his life, he was able to care for, and educate, over ten thousand children without asking a single human being for financial support, and leave a continuing legacy that would go on to reach more than one hundred thousand in the years that followed. George Müller believed that his calling was meant not only for benevolence, but to convince men that God is real and truly faithful.

"In the whole work we desire to stand with God, and not to

depend upon the favorable or unfavorable judgment of the multi-
tude."—George Müller

In the context of my struggle, I saw George as a rebel and a genuine fool for God, as one who in the face of criticism, opposition, and trials fearlessly and *foolishly* cut across the grain of sensible thought to follow God's lead instead. He tested the idea of faith by adhering literally to the promises made in Scripture and found that God is not only real, but absolutely trustworthy, and that God reveals Himself personally to men through His word and Spirit in order to accomplish His heavenly will on earth.

So at a time when my life was on fire, this moment was the fire sale where everything had to go, including my understanding of God, as well as my adultlike nature. After reading George Müller's testimony afresh, I decided then and there to see for myself—to find out once and for all—if living by absolute faith in God was truly possible for me.

It may sound foolish, but we see more clearly from the bottom of a well that every good thing comes from above. And this is where my journey in becoming an *extravagant fool* began.

My story, on the other hand, begins a bit earlier.

CHAPTER 2

DRIVEN

It is a wise father that knows his own son.
William Shakespeare, *The Merchant of Venice*

A HANDFUL OF RESTLESS

My earthly father never offered the words I desperately longed for, and that was hard for me. But as a high-strung son, I never offered him the patience to listen for them beyond the surface of his quiet exterior, and that was equally hard for him.

Consequently, my lifelong drive to establish my own value was equally perpetuated by these two opposing characteristics—digging impatiently for those missing words or acting on extraordinary impulse to prove my worth by exploring my potential in a host of foolish ways. Armed with an insatiable curiosity, I chose the second path more often than not, and the results are still speaking over my father's quiet love.

Yet as foolish as the ultimate result may have been, these

two aspects were simply parts of the "all things" spun beautifully together by my heavenly Father to help me know both of my fathers a little better in the end, and to finally understand that I'd always been known, valued, and loved by both, and that one of them had a plan. So I continue to thank them both today for what they've had to endure from day one as quietly active fathers with a restless fool for a son. A quick look back will offer a few laughs and illustrate how I became the wrong kind of fool.

> *A fool hath no delight in understanding, but that his heart may discover itself.*
>
> Proverbs 18:2 KJV

GOD'S CURIOUS PLAN

I'm sure my mom was joking when she wrote the words "This child is off" in the opening chapter of my baby book. But she was right. I was off indeed — off running from one room to another at the tender age of seven months. The real story, however, begins not with those early steps but with the fiery curiosity that propelled them.

After six years of freedom, the first day of school arrived like a prison sentence. There were thirty kids in matching checkered pants, and a middle-aged warden telling us where to sit. It took only a minute to see that the first grade wasn't for me. I raised one hand to gain the teacher's attention and held on to my pants with the other. She pointed me toward the restroom with a gentle push in the right direction, but I hooked a left at the water fountain and headed for home through the nearest exit. Three miles later, I reached my own front door and found that it was locked. Mom wasn't there to answer, no matter how hard I begged or how many times I knocked. She was actually at work, so I spent the day outside, and no one but my first grade teacher was even the least bit surprised.

By fourth grade we lived in a small house adjacent to several acres of green grass, and a good-sized Catholic church. The grounds were kept by an Italian man named Stanley, who was shaped like a barrel and stood about five feet tall. It was his opinion that the church was the house of God, and the grounds were God's alone to use. It was my opinion that unless God came out of His house to complain, He probably didn't mind a little football on the lawn.

Stanley was an older man who was not very fast on his feet, but he chased after us all, only to capture a stray ball on occasion and lock it away for keeps. On certain days during the summer months he would mow the entire property—half before lunch, and half afterward. This meant for a little while the mower was left unattended in the middle of our game field. It wasn't the perfect spot for an ambush, but with help from my dad's socket wrench, I loosened the back wheels faster than expected and dove in the bushes to watch. Stanley's reaction was priceless, a protest, evidently, that echoed a few choice words through the house of God. Only an Italian would know for sure.

On another occasion, while Stanley was off to lunch, I made my way inside the church to learn all I could about the power of holy water. Like the fountain of youth, it was right where I imagined, shimmering from a silver bowl deep inside the sanctuary. I was determined to be first among my friends to drink from it. But after one taste from what amounted to an indoor birdbath, I decided to sprinkle myself instead and run home before Stanley suspected a thing.

If curiosity tiptoes through a minefield, I was the kind of kid who adds a blindfold and music to make it more fun. I remember collecting cigarette butts from behind an old drive-in and smoking them with the unfamiliar people who called it home. That was the sixth grade. Later there were ringside boxing matches in the front yard, and roof-jumping contests with Mom's umbrella. There were hideouts in the woods, and pellet guns with live bullets taped on the end of the barrel. It was a time of believing in buried treasure, and digging to China to find it, until one early evening I found a dead body instead.

OVERLOOKED

I was off indeed — off running from one curious adventure to another. But something else was off that no one seemed to notice. Especially my dad, who was known as the strong, silent type — strong because he was silent, and silent because that's the way God made him. At least that's how Mom explained it.

By the age of twenty-one, I left for California with a close friend, a few bucks, and a simple plan. We traveled from Jacksonville (my home) to San Diego by way of Winnipeg — the extended route. Gone for months with little contact, we lived out of vending machines and an orange VW bus with a rusty floor and rotting orange curtains. We'd be surfing the best breaks from Washington State to Mexico, then set up life somewhere in between. With more than a few zigs along the way, we had a bona fide adventure. But at twenty-one, the farther you get from home the closer it feels to your heart. Familiar things have louder voices that never stop calling for your quiet return. And a few months in, we gave in to making a stealthy homecoming, hoping to surprise our families.

The outside of my parents' home was beautiful. I didn't knock. The only sound came from the lid of a boiling pot bouncing around, splashing the stovetop and foyer with balmy hints of dinner—Mom's dinner! I walked toward the kitchen, and there she was. Both she and my kid sister showered me with the extra-strength hugs that only a good surprise can muster. Lots of questions and stares—it was good to be home. No one knew when or if we'd be back, but there I was, and my father would be home from work any minute—I could hardly wait. Thirty states under my belt, chest out and chin in the air, I sat down and waited for him to step through the door. This would be better than scoring that touchdown on the very last play of my Little League career.

My heart leapt at the sound of the door pushing open. There he was. Dad walked right through and passed by his favorite chair on the way to the bedroom. Maybe he wanted to change clothes first. My eyes and posture followed him down the hall before easing slightly back. And my heart didn't give up because maybe he didn't see the kid sitting in his chair. Sometimes we overlook things we don't expect. But he changed his clothes and walked right past me again, heading for the kitchen. It was a silence that swept so hard against my youthful hope that it emptied me onto the floor. Two seconds and twenty years of second chances passed, and I left as quietly as I came. That moment was the culmination of two decades of waiting for those words, waiting for that look. It was the most painful silence of them all.

So it seems that slightly below the surface of boyhood curiosity there is a deeper ambition at work, one that mines every youthful minute for the treasure of one's own significance. The next twenty years of seeking approval left me bruised by hundreds of "look at me" exploits—from dodging the police in Rome to white-knuckled rides on top of the car at deadly speeds, from nearly drowning in the Irish Sea to ignoring instructions and skydiving my own way—and ultimately, from gambling my family on businesses and big houses to being emptied onto the floor once again.

If the faith journey is a minefield, then curiosity takes the first step and learns to tiptoe its way through. Pain, on the other hand, dons a blindfold and runs carelessly in circles without regard to consequence. The years leading up to my colossal failure were filled with curiosity and plagued with near misses, but ultimately driven by pain. I never rested or ever listened to anyone but myself. And I never realized that I'd spent my entire youth laboring to be found by my earthly father and laboring to resist being found by my heavenly Father. As a result, I charged ahead in my early career with a dangerous sense of invincibility and a reckless uphill drive. But in the rush of momentum that tackled each peak, satisfaction slipped through my hands the moment I arrived.

OVERLOOKING AND CONVINCED

One of the more humorous examples is when I worked for United Parcel Service, a company loaded with opportunity for advancement and a military toughness for following protocol. Simply play by the rules, and you will retire a millionaire— exactly what I wanted.

The facility was industrial and spread across acres of high-speed conveyors designed to reroute packages from one location to another. Most of my time was spent overseeing that process. Within a year, I was in charge of one of the largest operations in the building, accountable for nearly half the volume on my shift. It was an enormous responsibility that failing to precisely execute could mean six-figure losses in the span of just a few hours.

The environment was extremely fast-paced and highly stressful. Because of the intense pressure, there was a quiet tolerance among peers for anything that provided momentary relief, including the bending of certain rules. And there were plenty to bend or break, as long as you did it at your own risk. Tobacco chewing was the only forbidden fruit that I found enjoyable. From the top of the company down this was strictly off-limits. In my view the term "off-limits" simply meant "keep it inconspicuous." In other words, if I spit where it can't be seen, I won't get fired.

My area reminded me of a baseball field, but was approximately half the size. It had a ten-foot-wide observation deck mounted several stories above the floor for easy viewing. Unfortunately, its floor was made from grated metal, so hiding my habit took some ingenuity. The best method was an occasional plunk on the support post that spanned vertically from where I stood to the concrete floor twenty feet below. That way the evidence would hit the post and stretch its way down toward the ground but evaporate well before reaching it. So with a little help from gravity, my criminal activity was absolved and life was good. On the other hand, missing the target meant sending my dirty brown secret to an irreverent splat somewhere near the base of that post—a potential career-ending maneuver.

On a certain Friday when least expected, a national team arrived to observe and inspect the entire operation. Now, inspections were nothing new and generally came with enough notice to prepare in advance. A part of that preparation was ensuring that even the slightest details were perfected down to proper attire, paperwork, and especially avoiding any forbidden habits. The difference on this occasion was that the warning never came and one of the gentlemen visiting was a member of the UPS board of directors. During the inspection he and his team passed directly beneath my area without my knowledge. And by force of nature, the day that one of the highest-ranking officials had come to inspect my work, I missed the post and hit him directly on the lapel.

I now had the attention of my direct chain of command, a host of mid-level managers, and, unknowingly, the board member himself. After realizing that I missed the post, the crowd below came sharply into focus. With a chaotic surge of adrenaline my posture was snapped in the opposite direction. I looked away and then down at my feet, and finally, with a deep breath, took a broad survey of my glorious operation and pretended not to notice. But inching into my periphery like a column of finely dressed soldiers was the calamitous confrontation only seconds away. What I thought was a miss had clearly been a direct hit on the least familiar figure now leading the others in lockstep.

My own legs were locked at the knees and prickling as if every ounce of blood was attempting escape through my face. Even from a distance, I could feel the nauseating blur of their faces, clean shaven and dipped in stoic confidence like expensive cologne. And on the heels of the highest authority, they filed one by one up the stairs and into my domain. Without a word the board member looked me in the eye, then back at his thousand-dollar suit. A brilliant pin with his name and title were smothered in spent tobacco juice. There were fifteen people in all, huddled around in similar attire and held speechless by his every twitch. And every last expression was trained by the rules of engagement to conclude one simple fact — that I'd just been crowned king of all dopey terminations and was about to be instructed to pack.

With a nod at my employees and a two-second pause he laid a hand on my shoulder and spoke. "Kevin, your area is one of our best. You're doing an excellent job. Now, if you wouldn't mind wiping your spit off my suit, I'll convince these fellas to let you keep it." So there I stood, a young man with nothing but drive and a renewed sense of invincibility. Immediately after this rousing approval despite an apparent failure, I left that perfectly good career path still searching for a better pat on the back.

That sense of invincibility was a counterfeit hand on my shoulder that I eventually mistook for faith. Driven by pain and finding nothing but success fostered the idea that God was behind my every endeavor. The harder I tried the more faithful I thought I was, as my own strength seemed perfected by the ability to overcome any obstacle. The drive that began in curiosity might have killed me like the cat, but by a skewed interpretation of faith it had given me at least nine lives to throw away.

OUTDOING DAD

By my thirtieth birthday I had a new family, a multiple six-figure income, and the itch to strike out on my own. It was then that my boss of several years informed his employees that he was selling the company to a much larger one, promising that all would remain intact. They were famous last words that discouraged everyone but me. I was elated at the prospect, because it meant the time had finally come to step out in faith and start my own business.

My contract had long since expired, but as one of the top salespeople, departing to start a similar business kindled its legal wrath. The lawsuit was a groundless effort designed to slow my progress and make an example for others tempted to follow. I won the battle, but after a yearlong defense my new business had indeed suffered, forcing us to sell our home and nearly declare bankruptcy. From that point on there would be no satisfaction in simply regaining a good income. So I took on a partner and worked around the clock for the next two years in hopes of building a multimillion-dollar business, just as my boss before had done.

During this period I was introduced to a godly friend with a gift for creating custom software. With his help and inspiration, we set out to build something that would revolutionize our industry. As the project neared completion, I took the risk of hiring a sales staff and embarked on a one-year mission to develop our market. My original partner was unsure about the new direction and departed at what seemed to be exactly the wrong time — one month before winning our first small contract. But with the applause of wiser men, he decided the road ahead was a minefield that he and his young family needed to sidestep. For me, every ounce of risk secretly amplified my ambition to unearth the treasured sound of that one man's applause I yearned for. So my partner gave up his share, and I gladly embraced his decision.

Within that year, we gained additional ground through two new accounts, which attracted the attention of our largest potential client. Receiving a contract from the industry leader would ensure that their immediate competition would follow, securing for us a client base worth millions. But after months of negotiation, their lack of full commitment was finally revealed as a stall tactic. They embraced the idea, but rejected the hand that delivered it. Having seen enough to agree with its potential, they had seen enough to agree that re-creating the software on their own was a better investment. With a shoestring budget, backed by the equity in my house, taking a stand was a risk that even I was unwilling to pursue.

Ultimately, only a portion of the idea was ever re-created, but the perception was quickly adapted throughout the industry that our product was obsolete. Two years of effort and expense, along with any hope for its future, were tossed aside by our remaining clients. For me it was time to reconsider and take a deep breath.

FROM RESTLESS TO REACHING TO RECKLESS

On the other hand, the little engine who thinks he can, always believes he will. And so it all began again, without a flinch from my family or a word of caution from my wife. In a tearful downsize, I traded my downtown address and its people for a desk above the garage and a get-out-and-push style vehicle. We were broke for nearly a year, but still years away from being properly broken. I suppose that humility is a giant that only looks small to small people and men with little engines driven by approval. After a year of total commitment and seeing my family only as often as I saw their portrait on the desk, my income rose to its highest level. I felt more invincible than ever and listened even less.

Looking back on my youth has made it quite clear that time alone does not heal all wounds, and faith as a catalyst bears a striking resemblance to desire driven by pain. Ironically, neither will ever be found tiptoeing fearfully through daily life — something I refer to affectionately as "the minefield." The big difference is that faith charges ahead, trusting that any casualties are things we never needed in the first place, whereas desire without humility covers both eyes and rushes recklessly unaware. In other words, one runs with hope in the right direction, while the other only runs from despair.

Being driven by pain for a pat on the back is a story that took me forty years to write but only a minute for God to blow up and liberate my heart from its pages. Only now, facedown in casualties, am I able to clearly see that I was given the chance to surrender years before my defeat. But I cleverly ignored that gentle nudge, hoping for something out loud.

"I love you, son, with all my heart, and you have always made me proud."

CHAPTER 3

OKAY, GOD ...
IT'S YOUR MOVE

YOU'LL NEVER LIVE TO REGRET IT

By the end of 2004, my income rose to its highest level. In my own mind, I was a king, more invincible than ever. I took great pleasure in the sound of my own voice, while my soul festered in my confidence that a godly man is one who reaches his potential by providing all he can for his loved ones. I moved my family four times in four years—twice on the way up, bigger and better, at the speed of ballooning home equity, and twice on the way back to earth, including a damp, cold view of the street.

We'd lived in our original house for years, plenty of time for all five senses to recognize it as home. Simple, tastefully decorated, it had room for guests, a yard large enough for pets, and lots of quiet spots for time alone. While it needed updating and quite a few repairs, it was well built and had wonderful potential. In fact, we had stacks of notepads with planned renovations, even a few napkins penciled with what it might look like for the price of a little patience.

But our plans to fix it up fell flat, and our ideas for additions never took shape. We didn't have much of an appetite for updates, with an ensemble of bankers and financial pied pipers riding piggy on the backs of kings with big incomes. They were everywhere and I was listening to every note: "Don't be silly. Paying off the mortgage is a waste of capital. Be smart. Move up now and rent the place. In five years you'll have twice as much and never live to regret it."

So despite having the means to pay off our mortgage and live quietly ever after, we began searching for any excuse to get out of Dodge and live a little more like royalty. Honestly, the pickings were slim in "Leave It to Beaver" land, so we made up a few excuses and rhythmically chanted them to the point where plain old tomfoolery became self-fulfilling prophecy. Somehow we made it the neighbors' fault:

"I'm pretty sure the lady beside us hates our dog and is waiting for a chance to call the guys who euthanizes pets!"

"That hooligan next door has been emailing covert photos of our raggedy lawn shed to the homeowners!"

"I believe the neighbors hate our guts for refusing to drink crap beer and play Bunko. We need to leave this ghetto now, while we can!"

Sure enough, when our shepherd mowed down an elderly woman while on its way to a squirrel dinner, and she mentioned her attorney by name three days in a row, we poked a "For Rent" sign in the yard and hauled off with our dog and the rest of our possessions in the middle of the night. Finally we were off to the better life we all deserved and would never live to regret.

THE THRILL OF PARADISE

We moved for the same reasons as every other American — because we could. For my wife, we moved because of the overwhelming number of leaks and creaks. I was seduced by the devil in plaid on a showroom floor — "This baby won't last long." He was right, but for all the wrong reasons. Investing while my income remained high was the "every-man wisdom of the moment" with an "every man for himself" set of rules. Banks were giving away credit for houses as long as you could pay cash for the toaster. Homebuyers were knife-fighting with credit cards from SUV foxholes, outbidding one another by the hour from cell phones for a slice of counterfeit heaven.

On a lark, the year before, my bride went missing for an hour, lost in the wood-frame maze and unpaved roads of the promised land in its early stages of construction — now a bustling community with custom homes fit for a monarch, featuring built-in vacuums, flip-on fireplaces, and marble at every arm's length. Its perfectly planned randomness included a beautiful golf course, kitschy shopping, schools, churches, and the like, all built concentrically from the well-groomed fountain square outward.

It was paradise with a cherry on top, and we were hooked by the first few bites. Buying a house priced at four times our income seemed like a good idea, but always felt like a bad one, especially to my wife. Certainly the banks, staffed with church-going golfers and friendly faces bumping carts in the dairy aisle, were wiser and gentler than any loan shark from the borough.

So in the name of providing for our future, I entered the crime scene, choked wisdom to death, and shoved it in the closet, then washed my hands and rolled the dice in hopes of finding a better life—a bit of homespun nostalgia, Andy Griffith–style, without all the dusty neighbors.

Slam dunk, the neighborhood punk was gone, appraisals were soaring, and my ego was bowing in the roar of its own applause. I was the smartest guy in the showroom, with only a minor exception. To my Beverly Hillbilly surprise, we'd come under surveillance by the new homeowners association, which was carting about like a Gestapo meter maid ticketing for stray weeds, unapproved trim paint, and porticos with odd furniture. We were in trouble again, it appeared, but at least we were rich enough to pay for our weeds.

Within a year, the thrill and the dog were gone. Newer neighbors, professionals, celebrities, and gurus with tidy haircuts from all walks of wealth looked suspiciously the same as everyone else. So we moved again, three blocks up the hill and a half block below the largest home for miles, into an even newer, more prestigious home in paradise—about one-third larger and nearly twice the price. I was soaring on more business, more "blessing," more leveraged investing.

After landing another division of an already substantial client, I bought commercial property as well, bringing my portfolio to three homes, two rental investments, and a business condominium with ample room for a staff of twenty—even though I had only one. I suppose the spoils of victory, vision, and comfort will always belong to the tortoise, but the treasure of experience, reaching the end of oneself, and hindsight, hands down, belong to the hare. But until then, it was provision by leverage at light speed, and there was no turning back.

I continued on blindly until the day the phone r
October of 2008, and kept ringing—one call after another,
with clients telling me they no longer had the budget for my
services. When I'd finally been sucker punched by the truth,
just in time to watch the Enemy run off with my value as a
man—the ability to provide, protect, and please my wife. After
forty-odd years of being proud of my hollow accomplishments,
the emperor who had no clothes was all out of "hush" money.

LOOKING AT GEORGE TO SEE NOAH

It took a decade to build my ark and load up the family but
less than a second, it seemed, to blow it up and sink the pieces.
Hundreds of résumés had been launched like distress signals into the ethos of 2008. But nothing returned—no olive
branches or answers from God, and no calls from potential
employers. There was no escaping the cloud, and the rain continued to pour.

By 2009, I still had an immature faith and found it difficult
to be inspired by Noah or any other cartoon version of biblical
heroism. Of course, I never would have agreed with such an
inaccurate characterization. I loved the word and searched it
for answers regularly. But if I'm being honest, my actions up to
this point had been led by anything but God's Spirit, including
some very good things.

And because of my success, both in business, and as a
"Christian," not a soul knew, including me. I was a genuinely
good man, doing all the right things, especially in the eyes of
my Christian brothers. And if my ark hadn't been blown to
smithereens, I'd probably be trying to make it a little bigger, in
the name of Jesus. What I'm describing is an incredibly subtle

distinction between everyday faith that gets filtered by the cares of the world, and foolish faith—the kind that makes no sense to most people, and certainly the kind that Noah would have needed to do what he did.

So at the time, I was in need of a flesh-and-blood testi-mony—preferably this side of King James, not merely pointing to the word from a pulpit, but as one who fully experienced it. That is when God reintroduced me to George Müller, a young preacher from the nineteenth century, who offered such a testimony.

With his fearless resolve to live by faith, he accomplished the impossible. Anyone who can leave a legacy of food, shelter, and a Christian education for over one hundred thousand orphans without having asked a soul for a single penny is not normal. When we stop to consider that his *only* petition for support was to God, in a world bombarded by perfectly acceptable donation requests, well, that is *truly* remarkable.

George Müller made it simple. By trading his commitment to Christianity for an absolute surrender to Christ, he left me with a challenge: learn to live by absolute faith—foolishly so—and let the answers be the answers, unembellished by my own desires or the opinions of others. In essence, we didn't have to "do" anything with our circumstances except trust God for everything. Focus only on intimacy with Him, and He will do the rest—still an unpopular idea in mainstream Christianity. And at the time, still an unpopular belief with me.

Change was in the air, not just in my life, but in the world—a world I once thought I carried proudly on my own shoulders. The economic failure of 2008 revealed a great deal about the condition of God's flock. The time had arrived for many to take stock of what faith really means, or how literally we can live by it. It certainly doesn't happen overnight.

Throwing out all conventional thinking and simply trusting that God will feed the kids and keep us all warm isn't something we do, but something we embark on, a journey where we learn to live by faith — and nothing but — one frightening step at a time.

That process begins with humility, a quality that must be unearthed from the do-it-yourself stronghold that most of us call freedom — not with our words, but in our walk. Suffering is a must, and our first dose came by looking ahead to see that a lifestyle of day-to-day survival might not only be miserable, but could remain with us for years. And with no work to be found, even the prospect of mere survival remained a fragile one.

NIGHTMARE ON WILD ELM STREET

Our home was an all-brick, million-dollar house large enough for three families, and it still carried aromatic hints of oak floors and fresh paint. Construction was completed the year before, and we eagerly drained our entire savings to enjoy its roomy surroundings. But even before the drywall dust could be removed from those inconspicuous places, the nightmare on Wild Elm Street began without mercy in the world behind our faces — the unending stress over knowing what was about to happen and being helpless to stop any part of it.

Paying for that enormous house was impossible, but the nightmare was that it was impossible to stop thinking about it. The mortgage payment was the first thing to go, but all the other expenses, including homeowners' fees and upkeep, were next. Seemingly, there were as many costs involved as there were bricks that held the house together. After reaching the point of no return, we could feel the weight of every single one.

The days were long enough to hate, but passed quickly enough to be confronted endlessly by new phone calls and letters—and eventually by knocks at the door from men with badges. With every missed payment, the house seemed to grow larger, allowing us to spend less and less time together as a family. My wife and I needed time to process it all, but that process became isolation. Isolation became our refuge, and heaviness filled the entire new home until every square inch of it and those "new home" aromas made us sick.

Whether I was sitting in my car or my office, or sleeping on the couch, waves of depression came over me and settled between the silence of my heavenly Father and the boyhood jabber that filled the silence of my earthly father. I was all talk, and this time the entire world, including my wife, could see it.

Short reprieves from isolation brought long-winded conflicts between us about what to do and what not to do. George Müller must have been harebrained, because in the "real world," living by faith meant little more than burying our heads in the sand. Or so it seemed. Eventually my wife hated ole George, but only a hairsbreadth less than me. Her pain was wrapped tightly in the loss of control—the inability to plan the details of our basic needs. My pain, on the other hand, was royally enthroned on the opinions of others. Without a clue how long this might last, all final payments received from departing clients went to pay down business expenses, leaving much more than a livelihood and large brick home at risk.

Everything that was *truly* important hung by a thread.

After fourteen years of marriage spent working together, we finally gave in to working apart. Verbal declarations to

attorneys aimed at mutual protection—such as from bankruptcy—became silent threats aimed at self-preservation—
such as divorce. Individual escape was the latest bright idea.
I've always believed I could live in a box and eat Pop-Tarts
if necessary, as long as my family had somewhere else to go.
Equally ridiculous were the serious considerations we gave to
how one robs a bank, crashes a car to look like an accident, or
catches a fatal disease.

I suppose that idle hands rub raw the eyes of a desperate
man. Nights without slumber left nothing but sermons about
faith on the television and the wrangling strategies of how that
faith could work in my favor—even to the point of practicing
any New Age technique that promised some physical mani-
festation. Nothing materialized, and nothing depersonalized
my God as much as these futile attempts to rescue my family
without Him.

Since the idea of living completely by faith is a foreign concept to most churches, we began using credit cards to buy food,
clothes, and household goods. It was slightly more subtle than
robbing a bank, I suppose, but with nowhere else to turn—and
with God's people having offered their best advice—the kids
still needed to eat.

My teenage son was also hanging apathetically by that
thread. He never complained, and that was what scared us the
most. Teenage peers at best are a dubious replacement for a
family, and he seemed happy to live loosely according to God's
word. At the same time, our version of God was happy to press
him between its pages and walk away. It is an inadvertent legal-
ism when we teach a young man that reading the Bible is good,
but we forget to teach him that it can only be understood as
God intends—by faith through the Spirit's wisdom and

revelation. Apathy is a slow leak, easy to ignore but potentially very costly — a style of parenting that would cost us heavily in the years to come.

INCUBATING FAITH

But in these Job-like moments of apparent suffocation, the right idea of living by faith was only an embryo, incubating in the heat of our misunderstanding. Our girls, ages ten and eleven, were truly oblivious — happy, it seemed, to enjoy having their bedrooms the way they liked and having a dad still silly enough to do anything to make them laugh, like shouting whatever came to mind at our car's voice-activated GPS system.

"Do it, Daddy. Go on, say it!"

"Okay, okay — *pig fight!*" — only to have the car's foreign accent respond with utter confusion.

As the weeks passed and our frustrations continued and arguments intensified, it was as if God had His hand on our foreheads, waiting for us to stop punching the air and collapse from exhaustion. It was as if He was waiting for us to recall the joy of being childlike, where nothing but right now matters, and only those things directly in front of us have our attention. It was a bit like falling into a crevasse and coming to terms with how simple your future is — you're either going to die in that hole or count it the best day of your life when rescued.

Everything was equally polarizing and amusingly simple, including the housing market. Sell the house for enough to pay off the debt or lose it and be sued for the difference. We borrowed more than a million dollars in 2007 for that house, and it sold at auction for just over half that in 2009 — a simple idea that applied to every property we owned, all worth far less than what we owed. The nightmare on Wild Elm Street wasn't a nightmare at all, but the truth of our wicked economy and my failure to prepare in advance. But like angry children, we continued to fight with these inevitabilities.

HUMILITY BENEATH THE WEEDS

All things considered, our choices were limited to laughing, crying, or sitting idly while those around us went on shrugging their shoulders and living their lives. Fortunately, we still had the power to surround ourselves with different people, and attending a new church was one of the best ways to accomplish that. Sometimes it's easier to breathe where no one knows your story or the mess you've made of your life.

There we found people willing to help us without long explanations, though their help wasn't always a free gift. Often it came in the form of an odd job with a lesson attached — a different lesson, perhaps, from the one that God intended. Discerning the difference could be quite humorous, though I was thankful all the same.

One new friend with an overgrown farm had just such a lesson for this middle-aged idiot. In exchange for handling a few of my bills, he would gladly allow me to handle a few of his chores. The privilege was all his as he aimed to build my character by helping me see the value of working for a living. I was more interested in keeping the lights on at home than what he thought of my character, so I didn't bother to remind him of the expensive baby bed we'd recently given his wife without asking her to first trim our lawn.

The terrain on his farm was sloped and rough, especially near the entrance, and covered by dollarweed — too short to mow and too high to see the pea-sized gravel beneath. Now short pants are a lawn care must when a yard is small enough to mow in three passes, but I'd never even been to a farm, so I came ready to give my pale white legs some much-needed sunshine.

Manned with a weed trimmer the size of a small birdbath and some basic instructions, I was off. It was open season at the weed farm where hovering just above the ground, as if glued in place, were those little flat leaves that my friend was so eager to delegate to my care. After ten minutes in action I understood why, as the pea-sized projectiles beneath them were striking my body with each passing swipe. I sincerely considered tossing the trimmer aside, dashing into my jalopy, and punching the accelerator for all it was worth. Who needed electricity or a friend like this guy? Even his weeds were mocking me.

I might have wanted to leave, all right, but just as I reached for the trimmer kill switch, the crazy machine made a horrible noise and shut off all by itself. Considering what the farm owner already thought about my character, simply leaving it on the ground and heading for home would only prove him right, and certainly imply that I'd actually broken it myself—no thanks! I still had to face this well-intentioned soul in church. So if it was broken, with no way to pay for it, I'd have to stick around and attempt to fix it myself, which is exactly what I did instead.

The string had also been eaten alive by the rocks, leaving what amounted to a perpetually tangled mess. The repair took about twenty minutes, which gave me time to forget about the pain, and reconsider how much we actually did need the money. So with some conviction, I decided to stay and finish the job, at least for the moment.

The remaining work seemed insurmountable — acres of lush, green weeds with thousands of square-jawed little rocks screaming from below to be left alone. Within minutes my legs felt as if they'd been sprayed with buckshot from the kneecaps to the ankle bones, and my socks were soaked in blood. The longer it went on, the angrier I got — angry over the nonsense of being past forty with nothing to show for it — angry over weed-eating an acre of rocks to pay a bill. I hated myself.

"Lord, why do You want me to be in pain? Haven't I already been through this?" Even hoisting the giant trimmer violently into awkward positions failed to bring relief. "Never mind. You can't humble a man who's already on the floor, and I'm going to finish this, no matter how much it hurts." I believed intensely that my willingness to sacrifice was the root of true humility.

A few seconds later, a good-sized rock made a line drive directly into my forehead. I dropped the machine, dizzy from the blow, and didn't speak to God after that. But I refused to stop working, snatched the trimmer from the ground, and continued on until it shut off again.

In frustration, I sat on the ground and thought once more about leaving, but after glaring at the heavens and then back at the trimmer, I noticed my iPod right there next to it in the weeds, apparently having been thrown from my shirt pocket minutes earlier. I'd been so angry with myself that I'd forgotten to use it the entire time. But there it sat, ready to use, and without giving it much thought, I pressed play and finished untangling the trimmer line.

The song that played was not the one I expected, or remembered listening to, but I figured any song would be a good distraction at this point. So I restarted the trimmer, cranked up the volume, and went back to work, dizzy, bloody, and angry.

The pain intensified as new rocks pelted old wounds, but as the song played on, barely discernible through the whine of the engine, I began to sing and think about the lyrics. And through them God began to unseat the throne of my complaint with His thoughts—breathtaking thoughts of an innocent man being mocked, beaten, and spat upon, while remaining quiet. They were lyrics I'd heard a thousand times before, but never from the mouth of the only innocent man: "And though my heart is torn I will praise you in this storm."

Humility is the quiet resolve in the midst of unfairness, and it is never angry—a giant that only looks small to small people. I'd been crying so long for myself that I'd forgotten to cry for Him—for His pain instead of my own. Neither the hours it would take to finish, the red swollen mess it would make of my legs, or the "why me?" mattered for that instance—only the resolve to honor Him in the midst of it. With that revelation, I pressed on until the job was completed, no longer caring why the guy treated me like a kid by not just giving me the money.

I suppose if humility were a town instead of a man, it would be impossible to get there from here without trimming the weeds. At least now I knew which direction to start walking. At least now I had a map. And if there ever is a next time, I'll be wearing a pair of blue jeans.

Journal Entry #1

The best thing about a rodeo clown is that he shows us how a little less sophistication is downright respectable. The worst thing is that he has to get the crap beaten out of him to prove it. The more we learned that it was impossible to rely on the outside world as a means of escape, the more we found that having the respect of others is overrated. Fearless vulnerability works best when we give the world something to mock, but it's an art that, if perfected, nearly always ends in applause.

I was glad for the immediate provision, as well as the lesson. But honestly, I'm still about as humble as that rodeo clown with even less understanding, especially of people. Humility is the contact point for transformation and only comes through suffering—a bit of laughter mixed with many tears and the stillness that arrives in the midst of absurdity, when moving forward is not an option, or flailing about only ends in exhaustion.

Having His hand firmly on my forehead, waiting for collapse, and getting to an all-time low were good first steps in the right direction.

CHAPTER 4

IF THERE'S ANYTHING WE CAN DO

Journal Entry #2

It is far less painful to be beaten within an inch of my life than to be asked what I did to provoke it. It is far less painful to be robbed of every material thing than to be asked by a passing fool, "Don't you have work to do?" And it is far less painful to be left for dead by one who cares not than to be offered a loaf of bread on a chain from a loved one who critiques every bite.

ASKING GOD INSTEAD

Another new friend, one without a farm or a lesson to teach, had a bright idea to help us create something normally referred to as "extra income." To their credit, he and his wife provided food when we needed it most and least expected it — warehouse-sized bags of manna landed regularly on the steps without a

57

word. And what never mattered is that neither of them understood God's plan for us. What did always matter, however, was that they never once said, "If there's anything we can do, just let us know." They decided instead to ask God.

Good intentions, like air kisses, may shoot for the moon, but rarely if ever get beyond our own lips. If living by faith requires waiting on God, then giving by faith requires moving on His behalf, silently if possible. So when my trusted friend sat me down to explain the idea behind "extra income" — or any income at all, for that matter — I was all ears. He'd already demonstrated his own success, so it made perfect sense to listen, and ultimately to move forward under his tutelage and good faith.

My wife and I went to training conferences and were encouraged that our direction was taking a better turn, conferences filled with godly people who believe that abundance is not only okay with God, but his best intention for life on earth — something I wholeheartedly agreed with. Most of the people we met had years of wisdom and were sincere in their conviction. I felt right at home and decided to give it my all.

The work was simple — provide everyday products, items already in the cupboard, for people willing to buy them at a lower cost and better quality. We figured if people could see that I was working, trying to feed my family, they might be willing to buy from us instead of from the local grocer — at least a few items. With close friends and loved ones already aware of our circumstances, the most sensible starting point was to suggest it as a practical way to offer their support — nothing spooky.

The initial reluctance — and even a few cringes — reiterated the idea that asking "Is there anything I can do?" has become almost meaningless. We found ourselves affectionately insisting that food, clothes, and shelter was the only agenda. Cringes became friendly nods, and nods became stealthy exits. No harm, no foul—it was all just part of learning to live by faith.

IF GOD WON'T HELP, HOW CAN I?

On one occasion, however, that familiar cringe took a sporting leap over passive dismissal into downright mockery decked in a see-through suit. My friend and I traveled for about an hour to present a line of fitness-related food products to a gym owned by a family member. The good news, and the reason we took the trip, was because he'd decided to offer to his gym members the very same kind of products we were selling—supplements, protein bars, energy drinks, powders, and so on—as a means to increase his revenues.

After several folks from the gym tried the products, it was agreed we had something worthwhile to offer. We were excited for the opportunity and hopeful that helping him retail at least a few of those products would create some regular income for us both. At the very least, we could put a few items on display, and if they sold, we were all in business. If not, well, we gave it an honest try, and there would be no loss except the gas to get there and back.

About a week into the process, I received a call from the owner—a relative who was familiar with our struggle. He called to stop the initial order, which was a bit surprising considering our arrangement and that the cost was already covered. There was no cost to him at all, but he called to cancel all the same. His reasoning was clear, and I understood. They had decided to put something more well-known on the shelf. I was frustrated by the news, but it was his business, and that was his decision.

The problem arose when he asked what I was doing with my life and how I intended to support my family. He interrupted my answer, agreeing that it was a terrible time for many people, then rejoicing gleefully over having escaped it himself. As the conversation peaked, it started again from scratch. I kept asking him to listen—he kept telling me not to ask.

"Just give it a try with an item or two," I said one final time.

But his demeanor spoke louder between the lines, and I began to recognize what he was thinking. *Surely Kevin has something up his sleeve, a multilevel marketing shindig or two,* which he would only refer to as "trees."

After making our intentions utterly clear, no shindigs, just a mutual profit by making a few items available to his patrons, the conversation bounced back to how getting a job was a better option for me. I didn't bother trying to explain the obvious. Realizing that his joy over avoiding the worst economy in modern history would continue to drown out a family member's distress call, I was ready to accept our differences and move on.

Before saying good-bye, I asked a much smarter man than me for any other advice he'd be willing to share, being a very successful entrepreneur. His words of millionaire wisdom went something like this: "Well, I just thank God every day for blessing us so richly when things are so rough. Good luck with it. You've got my number. But keep this in mind—if God Himself isn't helping you, then surely there's nothing I can do."

By some Alice-in-Wonderland definition, I suppose he was right. I needed to ask God, not him. Even so, that's a bitter tonic to swallow. With a *thank you*, I hung up the phone and sunk to the floor, deeply hurt by the idea that the hand of God was a mystical force living well beyond the pockets of smart businessmen. "I'm selling protein bars because I can't afford groceries! Help me, God!" I shouted in disbelief.

If my own family was unwilling to help us unless God helped first, I was a bigger fool than either of us imagined. The next day brought a fresh start, along with an extra dose of encouragement from my extra-income friend. But the next few weeks brought even more rejection from those we never expected to cringe. Eventually, my friend and I agreed that God in His infinite wisdom must have other plans for me.

About six months later, that family member called and asked me how we were doing. "Struggling," I said. "About the same." Same truth, different day. After a brief pause, he offered me the opportunity to do some creative work for another one of his businesses, a charitable organization in need of a skill I'd become very adept at.

"I hear you're the best. This might be good for both of us," he said. Maybe this was his gruff way of helping us fill the pantry while providing something of value for the charity.

I agreed and spent an entire day on the project, not including the one-hour drive in both directions. The work required additional hours off-site, but I was only going to ask him for enough to cover my gas and buy a few groceries. When the work was done, he shook my hand and said, "Thanks a bunch for donating your time." Even with an awkward pause, I lacked the will to express my disgust or the wherewithal to at least ask for gas money—something I had to borrow in the first place. "At least it was done for a charity," I grumbled to myself.

Journal Entry #3

The climate is unfriendly for most, but most unfriendly for those who've been offered dramatically warm words on top of distant and dead deeds. To the traveler, beaten and robbed, "If there is anything I can do," says not the Samaritan, but the others passing by. "Just let me know, but if you do, I'm sure God will be watching over you. And rest assured that if He can't, then most certainly how would I ... help you?

Un-forgiveness, as equally destructive as greed, apathy, or misplaced judgment, was a real snake in the grass at my house for months afterward. I'm hoping it's not raising its head as I write. But the bottom line is this: Family or not, if the prescription calls for God's compassion instead of our own, it's likely that one of us never had any in the first place.

INHERITANCE IS A TRICKY ANIMAL

Eventually, as all the cringes became enigmatic shrugs, my résumés for corporate work became job applications for burger joints, and calls from all the wrong people never seemed to end—persistent gyrations from banks and credit card companies to us, our family, and even our neighbors.

And the more desperate our situation became, the less we found that we could count on the words of others, who were either cringing in self-preservation or shrugging us off in apathy. It was as if the body of Christ was being amputated right before our eyes, or dying, limb by limb, from atrophy. Reminding us, moment by moment, how many times we'd heard the phrase, "If there's anything we can do," and that gently nodding to let them off the hook was better than cringing ourselves over what they actually meant by it.

There were plenty of other circumstances where these delicate words were uttered, but only a few that made us bold enough to even reluctantly put our faith in the words of others by saying, "Actually, we *do* have a need—a big one!" As our mounting debts reached a critical mass, mounting threats with hints of dreadful repercussions forced us to consider where living by faith should end and the real world actually begins.

Having never defaulted or even been late on a payment in my life, hints about judgments, seizures, incarcerations, and the like were most perplexing, and mostly inconsistencies and collection strategies aimed sharply at forcing a reaction. Nevertheless, we knew not a willing soul with the resources to lend us through such bigger-than-life financial concerns, and we tried our best to ignore them.

Inheritance is a tricky animal with razor-sharp teeth and not something we desired to be standing near when it happened to someone close. But we were, and it did. The timing was severely ironic and made answering the "Is there anything I can do?" question glaringly untouchable. We didn't believe the world or any single person, even a blood relative, should be coaxed by guilt into spending a dime of their livelihood to bail us out of ours. And honestly, our kids had been helped in significant ways by this particular family-member-turned-millionaire well before their windfall. We were grateful for that and wanted no assumptions made to the contrary.

So at the point when most folks would say, "Loved one ... I'm in big trouble," we ran in the opposite direction—not in faith, but faithfully toward the altar of the fear of misconceptions.

We felt that by keeping a safe distance we could avoid any "reality-show family" types of misunderstandings, where self-preservation, assuming the worst of one another, and ridicule are forms of entertainment. No thanks—not for us! At least *that* was our strategy, until men wearing badges arrived at our front door to deliver legal documents that if ignored meant freezing even what little we had, or worse.

REVISING OUR EXPECTATIONS

Journal Entry #4

A new week brings us squarely into a collision that counts a little less than life or death but more than enough to garner a full-faced grimace from the average daredevil. The last bulb is burning out a mile inside the cave. There are no bread crumbs or Braille maps, only the hope that a final tap on the glass might offer a momentary flicker. God, I've done my best; please hurry and do the rest.

Spectators love to say, "God helps those who help themselves," or, "If you'll do your best, God will do the rest." But the closer we got to legal ramifications, the more preposterous that idea became. That clever "God is my copilot" thing that labors with gritted teeth to become a slightly better version of the early disciples is still never quite sure where faith begins and ends, and eventually screams, "Wake up, Jesus. We're about to die!" And the pendulum swings again.

What began with the fear of misconception ended in faithless desperation, shouting "Family overboard!" from the top of my lungs toward the only one around with a long enough rope to save us—a genuine blood relation who just happened to be a million times more solvent than me. Neither decision paid off.

The answer was yes ... then the answer was no. The loan amount was equivalent to several months of average household income—some of which we received, all of which we desperately needed. We were grateful to be thrown a life ring but we needed one with a rope. However, it wasn't cold feet or even concern about how we would manage, but the assumptions made about my character that ended up being used to explain the change of heart. Either way, the matter found a way to cause division between us for several years. As we took another step in "learning to live by faith," we learned a slightly different lesson. Yet it was still right between the eyes for the second time in a row, albeit a little less nobly than ole George Müller would have recommended.

If there's anything I can do.

Whether given or received, these words are worth nothing if not sincere. But they remain nothing special if not spoken to God on another's behalf and then acting on what we hear. Otherwise, whether we're afraid of giving away the storehouse or resolved to teach a man how to fish, we trade the voice of God's Spirit for an earthly brand of common sense. Certainly people should give or refuse to give as they see fit, but without the excuses we refer to as "lessons." The adages are what poison the water, but the silent gift and the honest refusal make everything sweet and clear.

Some would argue that in the real world, the good Samaritan wouldn't have helped the fallen man if he had found him again because doing so would have become too expensive. Others would say the fallen man, once beaten and robbed, has now been helped and needs to get a job. Honestly, we haven't a clue what the good Samaritan might do the second or third time around. But one thing I know for certain. A much better question to ask is, *How many times would Jesus help the man? Or, how many hungry people would He choose not to feed until they've learned how to fish or how to make their own bread?*

If living by faith requires waiting on God, then giving by faith requires moving on His behalf, silently if possible. Ultimately, we find that love is impossible in either direction without faith — faith that raises our expectations of God so we can lovingly lower them of people.

PART 2

CONFOUNDING
THE WISE

CHAPTER 5

EMBRACING THE MYSTERY

> When I was a child, I talked like a child, I thought like a child, I reasoned like a child. When I became a man, I put the ways of childhood behind me.
>
> 1 Corinthians 13:11

BETTER TO BE RICH THAN WISE

When I was a child, eleven to be exact, we lived next door to a Catholic rectory, home to several priests who presided over the church adjacent to our house. These men in black who smiled and waved but never spoke had an air of mystery that dignified them and took hold of my curiosity. My nosy nature was without a doubt a little mysterious to my next-door neighbors as well, as one summer morning, I decided to pay them an unexpected visit and ask a few puzzling questions.

After a quick knock from me at the rectory door, an elderly giant appeared from behind it. He was red-faced and grinning from one pocked cheek to the other, and the older of the two, who introduced himself while glancing at their lawn, just beyond my dirt-covered feet.

"Hello, young man. Bat Masterson's the name."

His hand, twice the size of mine, seemed suspended in mid-air from behind the all-black regalia and looked as if it moved independently from the rest of him. With my very best squeeze, I tried to make up the difference in size and told him my name was Kevin.

Informally Protestant and completely fascinated, I asked him questions ranging from *Do you have a badge and are you an agent?* to *How much would you pay for a crucifix made from Popsicle sticks and acorns?* Until finally, I asked the big one, straight from the physics book I got for a nickel at the book fair.

"Mr. Bat, do you believe that God can do anything?"

With only a hint of response, a light squint, and a subtle nod, he then waited, as if the "why" I was asking was the more important question. Although I was slightly distracted by a half-open door and the riddle of what I might uncover behind it, my first aim was to steal his black hat and stick it where he'd never be able to find it.

"Okay," I continued. "We're told that a man can move a mountain, but can God create a mountain so heavy that even He would be unable to lift it?"

Cleverly, he responded by uncapping my sweaty blond noggin and giving a nod to the lawn. With a plop on the head in one quick move, he'd stolen my hat and returned it with a five dollar bill.

"Could you help me out?" he asked instead.

He never answered my question, but I was better off without it. I mowed their lawn three summers on the idea that it was better to be rich than wise, but those tough questions have never escaped the grip of my fascination.

WE CANNOT FIGHT WHAT WE DO NOT UNDERSTAND

Better to be rich than wise — or so I thought. Ambition is a relative term, but for me it was the cart that I thought was a horse — three large homes, one business condo, my company's value, and every penny of a multi-six-figure income pushing its way through my character and eventually flinging it over a cliff. With monthly expenses in the tens of thousands and suddenly no income, gravity works immediately.

After reaching a point where our gritty circumstances became routine, we began to reason with God, contending fruitlessly for something tangible to fasten our grip to and pull ourselves in for a closer look. The most agonizing thing was thinking that He wanted nothing more to do with us. Or perhaps was only playing a wicked game of hide-and-seek with the answers and forever dangling them just out of sight. We cannot fight what we do not understand.

Journal Entry #5

A million-something in debt and no income is a life sentence without parole that settles like surprise on a hurt child waiting for his parents' reaction. Hemmed in and vacillating wildly between the A and B sides of the "life's unfair" anthem: "Why me? How can this be?" and "If I don't fix it, nobody will." Job's friends have come straight out of Scripture and gathered around to explain things. But all I hear is a chorus of bill collectors who couldn't care less about the mystery of it all. It's a double-edged struggle, where one side is the immediate pain and the other is the monstrous task of removing it. Things like suicide and bankruptcy make more sense than living in bondage for the next forty years. Working the rest of my life at an average job may end up being a blessing, but certainly not a solution. It's either time to give up or take matters into my own hands. Or perhaps it's time to change the record and play a new song. "Okay, God. What do You want 'for me'—from this?"

CHILDLIKE FAITH—A RETURN TO CURIOSITY

My oldest daughter, like her dad, has always had a curious heart, unafraid to ask and follow with a simple faith that the answers are waiting just around the corner to greet us. If something seems unreasonable, she's willing to believe it enough to challenge it.

"Dad, shouldn't we be praying for the Devil, since God is mad at him for all the bad things he's done?"

Or, "Mom, is the black box on an airplane indestructible?"

"Yes, honey, I believe so."

"Well ... why then isn't the rest of the plane made out of black box?"

At age four she came bouncing from the bathroom, dripping wet with tears in her eyes, to ask, "Daddy, didn't you say that anything is possible with God if you just believe hard enough?"

"Sure, sweet girl. Absolutely."

"Well, Daddy ... I've just come from the bathtub, and it was filled up to the top."

"Uh-huh." I suddenly imagined myself backhanding the

floating chairs, toilet seats, and toothbrushes half submerged in Bathroom Lake.

"Daddy?"

"Yes, sweetheart?" I'm now reluctantly reaching for the bathroom door, with her close behind me.

"Well, um … I've been trying and trying to walk on the water the whole time, and I just can't do it. I'm really sorry, Daddy. I believed I could do it with God's help, but I can't—and I'm really sorry."

With profound silence, I looked at her curious little face and hoped for a routine word, but only routine things came to mind: *bubble baths and deep puddles, stains on the kitchen ceiling below, fresh folded clothes that were already way too small, and beds crammed full—above and below—with stuffed things that always had to go before bedtime. And plenty of routine answers for daughters under the age of five.* But all I had to offer this time was a hug—one I couldn't let go of without a little extra help from above.

Help me, Father.

Just one thought that gently brought the next one: *Anything is possible with Me, but not everything is useful to Me. Peter only walked after I said, "Come."*

"Sweet girl," I said on the heels of that thought, "it is possible for you to walk on water, but only if it's something God wants you to do. Did He tell you to walk on the water?"

"No, Daddy, He didn't. I just wanted to."

Before I could finish that brilliant thought, though, she was on to the next subject. And I was left with yet another routine floor to clean, as apparently *both* of my daughters had given that particular miracle a try.

It took four towels and five minutes to absorb the inch-deep pond that led to their bedroom—just enough time to consider with a snicker the audacity it takes to submerge an entire room with water and attempt to walk on top of it. And just enough time to be reminded that reckless curiosity may spoil the environment but has a way of getting to the point—like the child willing to challenge a priest by insulting his faith and ultimately winning his affection. The apple had fallen close to the tree, and had rolled off into the same deep grass that eventually begs to be mowed for one reason or another.

I wondered what that priest might say to a fortysomething about to be forced from his home with no income or credit, overwhelmingly in debt—a man still curious enough not to lie down and die, but bruised enough not to willingly stand up and walk in the wrong direction. Another plop on the head would be best, another five-spot to settle the matter, a small bribe that moved a mountain of logic by faith, his faith in my ambition at the time, his faith that God is never silent by accident, even if it takes thirty years of misguided ambition to uncover it.

MORE TO THIS LIFE

The longer I pondered the idea in the context of what others were saying, the more I realized that what we were living through couldn't be fixed, nor should it be. Mysteriously, my career, savings, investments, a company built from scratch, our home, and nearly all that filled it had all been scraped from the surface, until even the deeper freedom that these things provide became superficial, almost meaningless.

Still, all the answers from those around us pointed in the same direction, indistinguishable one from the other. *Do more, prepare more, become this, give that, be more committed.* It was a litany of *do, do, do*, until even despair goes blue in the face from loitering outside the window and being ignored. We were less interested in how to get our life back than in what "more to this life" actually meant.

The inclination of mature thinking is to provide sophisticated answers for age-old ideas, to lean on our own understanding while calling God the genius behind it. "Kevin, dream all you want, but mountains don't literally move, and you've still got to put beans on the table!" But the genius of God is mustard seed faith — the childlike willingness to embrace a mystery by believing it just enough to continue challenging it, like a poke in the back from God that persuades us to revisit our contempt for the familiar.

Journal Entry #6

Two guys sitting on two rocks two hundred years ago.
    One says to the other, "Anything is possible!"
    The other says, "What do you mean?"
    One says, "Man can fly."
    The other says, "It's impossible ... I've already tried."
    On the one hand, a man must literally become a bird to fly. On the other hand, a man can fly by the substance of things hoped for, the evidence of things not seen, faster and higher by faith than any bird has ever dreamed. Perhaps the mustard seed in the spotlight casts a mightier shadow than expected. Apparently, I've fallen asleep on the front-row seat in the shadowy comfort of my own understanding. The power of God lies not in the size of the seed but in the gigantic potential He's hidden within it — the Harvard degree in faith that will rise to the top of the industry if we'll stop attempting to dig our way out and just plant it.

So no more talk of beans, please. We have a mystery to unravel. Not how to repair the wreckage or even how to pilfer beneath it for food, but uncovering instead what good thing God desires to teach us through the experience. Just a friendly game of hide-and-seek, where God holds His good plans in the heavens but tucks Himself just out of sight. We faithfully count with our eyes closed, while He anticipates the ready-or-not moment, only to delight in our search from behind the curtain while his child tiptoes nearby. I'm only good for one or two rounds of hide-and-seek with my kids, but when my daughter counts to ten and then comes running, my heart skips a beat every time. And I wait eagerly for the sheer joy of embracing her in laughter as she gets to win the game.

We always win with our heavenly Father, but the mystery may be the only way He can get us to participate. We go looking for the better answers, the deeper things behind the obvious, the truth about His character — and find Him instead, waiting and ready to embrace us. The depth of God can only be revealed by the personality of God. I believe God smiles when we challenge Him with our flimsy logic, like a young boy who challenges his father with a flimsy rubber sword. It's not insulting; it's endearing. But growing up means giving logic the cold shoulder and becoming intimate with the One who puts the beans on every table. It requires the willingness of a child and the vision of an adult. We don't have to labor over it like an odd puzzle piece, and neither do we have the right to dismiss it as useless. What we knew as children we were learning again as adults — how to embrace the mystery of our very grown-up circumstances.

CHAPTER 6

THE HOMELESS LANDLORD

GAMBLING WITH LIVES

I recall the excitement of pressing ink to a stack of paper and humorously contemplating the simplicity of wealth. Squiggle the hand about for a minute or two, and — presto! — keys to "the kingdom" would slide across the table like a short stack of brass poker chips.

But sometimes God ducks in the side door of a life as if it's a seedy casino and turns over every last game table. And foreclosure — the first of several — brought the oddest sense of satisfaction, a kind of *C*-minus victory celebrating the defeat of one's own flawed character and the realization that it was better for a man to have his empty pockets torn away than to continue to fill them with empty promises. No more gambling with lives. No more buying houses.

The revolting imbalance between what we owed the bank for our home and its updated street value was condemning evidence that shylocking was corporately legal, and breaking financial backs. Along with our original down payment plus equity, the bounty price for my intelligent signature was in the neighborhood of a half million dollars in just over a year. More importantly, with both rental homes occupied at break-even rates, now equally upside down, without a stitch of income, cash, or credit, we literally had nowhere else to go.

Adorned in expensive coats, preheated cars, and posh advice by satellite, we looked the same, dressed the same, and waved at the same neighbors. But underneath we were shivering with an invalidity that no one else could see, including our local tenant. We may get those Pop-Tarts after all and attempt to make a home from the box.

A NEW BRAND OF LANDLORD

Journal Entry #7

From rainy day investor to homeless landlord,
I was steering the ship from a life preserver, with no
     way back on board.
I cut adrift my family's dwelling and sentenced them
     to the street,
but anchored a mansion for my tenant, who offered
     us nothing but grief.
He never took a second look, nor would he ever
     agree,
that through my empty pockets the ground is all that
     you see.

For a moment, we were stuck without a home, and our tenant was stuck without a heart. While considering how to parcel out my family to live with friends and neighbors, we surrendered our home, with no assets, income, or method of retreat. Yet by some "house of card" irony, we were still shackled to a waterlogged investment—a rental home with negative equity and Yosemite Sam for a tenant. With all the sad folks sleeping in alleys and underneath bridges, how many possibly owned a rental home? Would I be the first? Could I live in a box while my tenant summoned me to fix the plumbing?

With a cup of coffee and a worried look, I shared the news with our tenant. Without a word, he shook my hand and headed for the exit. But seconds before he shut the door, he turned and said with a stubborn stare, "I will sue you, mister, if you sell my home. Just making you aware." Before any rational response made its way to my lips, Yosemite reached for the extra-long door of his white Jaguar—the same one I supposed that he'd be driving up to my mattress to pay rent. The news was simple, really. I had to sell, so I offered him the house for less than we owed. But I reassured him that if he chose not to buy, his lease was still intact with anyone who did. And other than showing the property with plenty of notice, this wouldn't affect him at all. The only measure of protection for either of us would come from the hands of a new landlord—not a homeless one. But he didn't want to buy, and he didn't want me to sell. I had gambled with his life, and for that he was content to leave me in the well.

When a rainy-day investor begins to chase a storm, occasionally that storm reverses course and begins to chase him. It certainly wasn't the odd rationale of my tenant that caused our circumstance, but now it sat like a heavy object directly on top of our escape hatch. His rationale was a mystery to me, like a thousand-piece puzzle with no picture or box. I didn't know where to begin or where it might end. But it didn't end there. Yosemite's belligerent bag of tricks included legal letters, bitterly critical emails, intimidating potential buyers, and late, partial, or unpaid rent—which by that time wouldn't cover our costs. This was the climate of our relationship for the next several months.

There are differences between considering how it feels to be homeless and thinking through how to live without a home. There's the immediate confrontation of the "how to" and the urgency of your answer. But the big difference is realizing there is no retreat. It's not about selling wedding rings or living with friends for a moment; it's about looking out ahead of you and seeing nothing on the other side. It's the nightmare that looks simple through a keyhole, but entirely different through the holes of empty pockets. Every hopeless glance at the bed of a tired friend looks more like the back seat of your car, and eventually the alley where it was parked. I'm not saying I've been there, but we *had* to go there in our minds. You can only watch it through the keyhole until the bank changes the lock—and they were on the way.

FREEDOM BY SURRENDER

It seems that miracles most often occur in that blink between surrender and captivity, so we had to be homeless in our minds before appreciating the home God had in mind. And from the smallest, most unassuming place, He opened the window of humility and blessed our willingness to climb through it.

My wife had previously checked on a few small rentals. Amazingly, in spite of us having no credit or income, we got a call from the motherly landlord of the smallest one. She said God had spoken to her about us and the place was ours for the next year. She broke all the rules and took us in, based on her faith and our word. So the new landlord we'd been praying about was meant for us, not my tenant. We moved in without the slightest idea of how to pay the rent, but within a week God provided a small project and several odd jobs that covered our living expenses for the next few months. At least we'd have a place to hunker down and untangle the mess.

Through this blessing, our tenant, a man who relished the idea of his landlord becoming homeless, had no further influence over our reactions, character, or living arrangement. But that declining influence brought more frequent and desperately sharper criticism from him. So we thanked God for giving us a place to breathe, but we thanked Him even more for the revelation we received as a result. For our battle wasn't defending against the barrage of criticism from our tenant, but in learning to forgive him for every ugly word.

GAMBLING ON GOD ... INSTEAD

Continued forgiveness is unwillingly attached to ongoing persecution—but it's attached for good reason. As we approached the home stretch of our tenant's lease (final month), things got very quiet—no more nasty emails or threatening letters, just silence. With a month to go and out of curious concern, I emailed to remind him about vacating. A few days later, the response email arrived from his address:

> My husband was diagnosed with liver cancer this year and it has now spread throughout his body—advancing to stage four. He's lost 50 pounds in the last two months and is no longer able to walk. His business has suffered, and because of pre-existing conditions, our medical insurance is not covering the costs. There's not much more we can do.

My overwhelming impression was concern. I wasn't shocked or feeling shame for having been frustrated — just concerned. Somehow it was terrifyingly beautiful to recognize that a dizzy man was about to fall, yet God had His hand in the small of his back for an instant. It's that very moment when He leaves the ninety-nine for the one — the one who'd already lost his balance by the edge of a cliff. I've heard it said that we should preach without words because actions have much greater volume, but sometimes quiet words are the only actions loud enough to reach the ears of a plummeting soul. My last reply would be the sturdiest rope I could toss.

> I want to tell you that Jesus loves you, my friend — so much more than you will ever understand. He made you to be loved and you are the jewel in His crown. He gave you His heart by dying for you as you are. He is our only hope, the only One who can lift the weight of our sin and remove it forever. If you haven't given Him your heart, the time has come.
>
> — Praying for you.

His response by letter was brief, but sincere. "Thank you, Kevin. Your kind words have meant so much to me."

Weeks later, the house was vacated, with the exception of a few personal items, stray golf clubs, framed certificates, plaques, and a toolbox full of tools. It appeared that friends had moved his things a bit haphazardly and left some behind. I may never know if he accepted the invitation, but at least he was given the chance. And maybe now we both had a heart, and hopefully a peaceful home.

A few months after the letter, his obituary arrived in the weekly news and offered an equally black-on-white perspective, leaving a question that is easier to dismiss than answer honestly, but one we will never forget: *What would we be willing to surrender if it brought salvation to one lost soul—a paycheck, our home, maybe even our livelihood?*

It's one question we may never have to answer, but at the very least we will always continue to ask, at least as long as we care more about our own temporary needs than the eternal needs of others. There is only One who saves, but we are the ones who point the way—unless we let other things get in the way.

When I look back on the frustration and hurt this man caused, I have to remember that it must be only a fraction of what he was feeling himself. If we hadn't suffered the loss of our home or forgiven his anger, we might never have known of his pain or taken the time to share the good news. If the One who inhabits us considers one lost soul as priceless, maybe we should too.

Journal Entry #8

Good news falls with greater purpose on the spot
   where God takes aim,
But evaporates on that empty surface if we're
   chasing bigger drops of rain.
Yet even an ocean of stolen drops won't drown that
   still small voice
As it calls for all the drowning lambs to at least be
   given a choice.
And every martyr bleeds for what each brick in every
   church demands,
That we stop dragging the wealth of Egypt across the
   desert sand.

Making every provision a tool for harvest distinctly
    where we stand,
And watch the good news honor God for the sake of
    one lost man.

CHAPTER 7

NOT "THE PROVIDER"

Journal Entry #9

*It's "embrace a mystery day" at our house, and I
   smell smoke.*

It's either fire in my spirit or the burning of my hope.

*The enemy's bound at the window, but he's blocking
   all the light.*

*He's shouting, "Be still and panic. Your God has left
   you in the night."*

Your lily of the valley died forever on that hill.

*Now unbind me and I'll help you cope with a handful
   of pills.*

*C'mon! Your bank account is empty and your mind is
   full.*

*The tug-of-war doesn't end just because you've
   decided not to pull.*

ING ON MY BOOTSTRAPS

I once thought greatness was measured in a husband by his ability to provide and his willingness to please his wife. By this long-standing belief, I'd been inadvertently seeking the kingdom of "all these things" instead of the King, who is more than happy to provide them. Despite the willingness to embrace my dilemma, I was only maintaining a flexible faith, the faith of a man who believes that God is more powerful than himself, but not quite as smart—a faith where small victories are quickly hijacked by the Enemy and used to disguise the overall solution.

The truth is, I hadn't been able to provide for a while, but until God revealed my error, I considered that inability only a temporary setback. While resigned to never again having anything of great material value, I'd never lost my commitment to provide life's basic necessities. After all, anything less would make me anything but a decent Christian husband. But with no end in sight, no possibility of maintaining even that fragile nobility, my identity as a provider finally choked on its own bootstraps and breathed its last. So it's from the throes of absolute inadequacy that revelation arrives. Only where commitment to godly things fails can surrender to the God who provides them begin to thrive.

CHIEF OFFENDER OF THE MIND

The bank sold our home for half the amount we paid, and my wife, incredibly frustrated by the experience, had her eyes on a particular rental. But God stepped in and offered more than just a refuge for our large family. We settled instead into a tiny rental with a moldy campground bathroom and a perpetually broken air unit. It was perfect for us, and we hated it.

She referred to it as an "ugly plaid shirt two sizes too small" that God insisted she wear. I call that "throwing a fit," but I couldn't blame her because the responsibility was entirely mine. God made it clear that we were to move in for a time to adjust our thinking and renew our minds. We stayed, and she made it a home.

Several months later in the deep summer, about midday, I fell asleep on the couch. It was a long morning of old coffee and reheated résumés—one after another—ninety-five degrees outside and at least one hundred in the house. Caffeine is no match for the snake charm of monotony, but I didn't care. Falling asleep midday was my way of feeding the pigeons from the park bench instead of working. Or maybe God still had His hand on my forehead, waiting for me to stop punching the air and collapse. Either way, stress hung in the air and followed me everywhere, including my sleep, mocking my failed attempts to find work.

The dream was vague, but I remember vividly the stressful image that ended it. My kids had recruited my wife and me to play kickball (something we did on occasion to spend time together as a family). It was late in the afternoon, and we were playing in an overgrown garden with a flat, grassy field at its center—like something you'd see on the grounds of an abandoned estate. There was ample room for kickball, as long as the adults didn't kick the ball too hard and send it flying into the bordering brush, and who-knows-where beyond it—which is exactly what I did, only to watch my entire family chase after it at full speed and quickly disappear into the brush. When they didn't return, I ran after them and stopped just before I realized we'd been playing on top of a skyscraper, and there were no railings.

I was awakened by blood pressure telegraphing distress signals to all parts of my soul. Obviously it was stress, but the impression it left was vivid enough to reconsider that something more meaningful had occurred—a lesson perhaps from the Chief of Peace, who is equally known as the Chief Offender of the Mind. A garden spoiled with chaos, my own high altar of misplaced intentions, a green-space-gone-war-zone, with a solitary thing to preserve—my family.

God is weird, but His strange impressions tap at the glass until we're annoyed enough to look up and begin to truly listen to Him. The counterfeit idea says the dream was just fear over losing my role as provider and protector. But in the context of counting it all joy, the dream was a message that said, "Kevin, you were *never* the provider or protector, so let go already." The difference is subtle and slick enough to knock any average Joe just out of parallel until eventually he's moving in the opposite direction. I'd become a man ready to embrace the mystery of my circumstances, but unwilling to let go of everything—a man still white-knuckling his perceived identity, by failing to abdicate his family from a throne meant for a king.

SELF-PORTRAIT

With little else to do, I prayed for the first time in months—I mean really prayed, without groping for meaningless words aimed only at wearing God down. *"Father . . . I know that You're here . . . but I don't know what You want! So speak to me! If You want me to understand . . . just speak to me—please!"* I cried out to Him, knowing that unless He shatters the glass and rescues my heart, it will always be window-shopping for His presence. And then I spent the afternoon at the one job He'd given me — that of digging into the only other garden that came to mind, spoiled by the same mistakes, and uncovering an eerie self-portrait.

In that portrait I saw a man like Adam, who sat down when he needed to stand, who in the name of avoiding conflict traded God's applause for his wife's. Eve was tempted by knowledge, but Adam was tempted more by her appraisal of him — leadership by the law of "if Mama's not happy ..." Maybe the world has reduced this event to a cartoon script where sneaky teens get backhanded by God for wanting a little more knowledge. But even as a believer, who understands that Adam and Eve both bore the responsibility for their sin, I failed to recognize that Adam, in the context of his leadership role, bore the ultimate responsibility for allowing this event to happen. It's obvious, though, that Adam should have said no, and instead led his wife in the opposite direction, because as the shepherd of his family, leading them to follow God was his number one responsibility. And the rest, I guess, is history.

IF YOU SPEND IT, MORE WILL COME

Holly and I were married at twenty-something, she with a young son and me with a budding career, and we both came to the marriage with a better than average sense of frugality. Whether searching the couch for change or paying off student loans ten years early, our desire was to save, and our bent was not to waste. As a result, we entered our thirties with a house full of kids, zero debt, and plenty for shakes and pizza. During the second year of marriage, my income tripled, allowing her to stay home and me to set my sights on tripling it again, a feat I accomplished by the following Christmas — and what a Christmas it was. Home videos from that year are the best evidence that our kids were angels on a hayride to spoiled-child hell and utterly thrilled that Disney was along for the junket.

We suddenly had the income of a doctor without the twelve years of discipline or mammoth debt from med school—and an endless supply of fuel for shopping, high-end hairdos and makeup, New York Strip and swordfish, better cars, longer vacations, and larger homes with bigger, better furniture and plenty more hip feng shui trinkets on the walls. This was adulthood, and it came easy, so easy that years of baggage stayed buried beneath it with our frontal lobes stuck on misfire. No matter how much came in, we both found a way to spend it.

She bought small things frequently and I bought big things occasionally, so it all evened out and evenly hollowed out our conversations that surrounded it—gaping holes that ended in short phrases such as, "I don't know," and "Oh, nothing." We went from onetime spendthrifts with a sense of purpose to directionless apathetics junked up on what we thought would look good in a room. Or better yet, "Let's renovate that half of the house since we can afford it."

If you spend it, exponentially more will come. Spend five hundred, and twice as much will show up on the next paycheck. We were miserably thrilled at the prospect of bottomless-pit freedom; I was even more thrilled that it all came through my proud-provider hands. Holly's quiet pain of needing to feel worthy collided with my never-shut-up need to feel important, and melded into one long, redundant note played from our single-string perspectives. Money gave us both small victories. It kept me from picking the scab and her from turning her back and sweeping herself underneath an already lumpy rug. Or so we thought. Actually, all we knew was that buying more made

us both feel better. I was skin-deep happy when she .
ing, but underneath we were both gritting our teeth.

My bull's-eye perception of what Holly wanted and needed
was dead center on the wrong target. She needed a partner
secure with himself, more than one who offered himself as
her security. But we never could get that established, so life
went on with the same song left on replay for years. My version: "If Mama's not happy, nobody's happy." Her version:
"Mama's not happy, but Papa won't shut up long enough to
find out why."

I CAN SEE WHY

Adam should've said no to Eve, and Kevin Adams no to his
misconception. But after fifteen years of marriage I can see why
neither of us did. Nothing on earth moves me like the encouragement of my wife, and nothing can injure me like her shame.
By design, she has great influence in my life. If she is close to
God, that influence becomes an extension of His hand. But
if she is operating from pain or some other contingency, that
influence can become a weapon of the Enemy.

Ultimately, in that same self-portrait, I saw a saved man
assigning himself godlike value for his ability to provide. But
it was actually a curse worn in the flesh like a badge. When it
was ripped away, I suffered because I'd forgotten the truth. My
value is measured by the price that was paid for me, not by the
sweat of my brow or career status—a truth that is easy to say,
but hard to accept.

So I'm "not the provider," and never was, a revelation that
liberates the spirit but hogties the natural mind. An acquaintance rebutted this thought by quoting 1 Timothy 5:8—"A

man who won't provide for his family is worse than an unbe-
liever." "Kevin," he said, "your argument goes against Scripture
and gives license for men to do nothing." I responded in kind.
"I understand, but what men do or don't do is an issue of the
heart, one that doesn't require a license from me. I'm not referring to a *willingness* to provide, but rather a bent to replace God
with my own strength."

Besides, the context of that verse is completely focused on
grown children caring for widowed parents—"family that has"
helping "family that has not"—expressly those in our immediate family. It's a bit of a stretch to use it another way, especially
to condemn a man seeking God with all his heart for direction.
Regardless, I need to stop placing my value on anything except
the finished work of the real provider.

IF *ABBA'S* NOT HAPPY

Journal Entry #10

Whether men hold court by the sweat of their brow or
women glory in the ability to subdue it, these cross-broken
curses perpetuate without mutual willingness to abdicate
the king of all slings and his bucket of mud:

- The wife falls into the trap of relying more on the
  husband than on God.
- The husband relies on his ability to provide rather
  than on the provider Himself (God).
- The wife undermines the husband's authority by manipulating his desire for her approval.
- The husband receives affirmation by satisfying his
  wife's desire instead of God's will.

My wife is my best friend and most forgiving adversary. Moving her into that tiny rental was like insisting she make a home for five in a hollow tree trunk meant for gnomes. And to be fair, we did have to wedge our couch between the living room walls by force. The kitchen had buckets of dust and cramped appliances held together unintentionally by old Crisco and a little bad eyesight. The bathroom had broken grout that smelled of briny bath slippers, and wallpaper three layers deep, apparently left by Eleanor Roosevelt. It was too small, too geriatric, too humid, with far too many leaks and noises, way too ornate, with too many kinds of paint. Ultimately it was my bride's own grubby version of a Pop-Tarts box with four beds, two baths, and a sink. But it was also the pride and joy of a tenderhearted widow who cared more about our welfare than our credit score and, therefore, much too good to pass up.

We both knew the decision was right, but it needed a spark of leadership from a husband who was learning to put God on the throne instead of his wife — an idea that never occurred to me until being interrupted from feeding the pigeons with a dream and a dose of His word.

In a transformation by inches, this was a good first step with a little fine-tuning. Proving more often than not, that God's work is slow and deep while the Enemy's is fast and shallow. Where my commitment to God had failed, my surrender to Him was beginning to take root — bearing the fresh fruit of intimacy and a new childlike recognition of His voice. I was never meant to be the provider, but only the conduit through which God provides — a big difference when it comes to handing out glory.

The old catchphrase "if Mama's not happy ..." is the echo from a dusty garden spoiled by the greatest mistake, a poison fix that keeps wives miserable and husbands intoxicated, numb to the subtle exchange of glory that occurs when we think of ourselves as "the provider." Bottom line, good fruit is born, not produced — and if *Abba's* not happy, neither will anyone else be.

CHAPTER 8

THE "KNOCKOFF"

HOPE SPRINGS

Two months to finish this book on two weeks' cash, no experience, and a wife learning not to flinch — I wonder how it all unfolds, and how she's been unfolded like fresh linen, preparing our table with no food in sight. "Just write, honey. Just write." I think back on the sleight of hand and slung mud that wrapped us tight and held us together, a few of the "all things" that have worked together to grow something better from the whole — two seeds tossed in the same hole, tangling toward the surface by struggling through every dirty inch.

FROM OUR OWN DIRT

Only two years into our marriage, Holly was pregnant with what would be our youngest son — a girl they initially told us was a boy, but a child with only half a chance to be anything

95

but a painful memory. She had renal failure—two bad kidneys that we thought of as some kind of unholy retribution for our ignorance. Perhaps it was the result of our fighting over less important things—me pushing her to open up, and her exploding on occasion. Or maybe it was that time that I pushed with my arms, instead of words. Physical expressions of anger were rare, but it would've been dishonest to dismiss them, especially when a child's life hung in the balance.

Either way, the baby wouldn't survive without immediate surgery, and even that might not prove enough. Twenty-three months of becoming familiar with one another, five months of making plans, four months away from a devastating end—the birth of a dying baby and contempt the size of her father's ego, which was an enemy target so big we could make it a home and still forklift in the pallets of unlearned lessons behind us.

After her incredibly lengthy surgery to remove all of one kidney and most of the other, our daughter pulled through and was healthy within weeks. But my false identity would take ten more years of ego-driven commitments—worldly appetites trapped in Christianese sentiment, to be revealed as a fake. Striving for years to be a good husband made me feel like a leader, but without the lead of God's Spirit, we ultimately found ourselves crammed in a tree, physically drained and complaining, and not a square inch to spare for two spouses with a lifetime of baggage.

The home had just enough wrong to strip our souls bare and show us what we really cared about. It certainly wasn't the fungusy floors, yard gnomes, or gazing balls; nor was it the light pink bricks that bordered every tree, flower, and even a few weeds. It was nice if you're old, we supposed, and a blessing, if you're nice enough to lie. As a failed provider, I was presented with the perfect time to consider the lilies, but as a leader, I just kept mowing the hell out of them in frustration.

Somewhere between no longer being "the provider" and never having been "the best leader" I was learning the hard way that there's a subtle difference between a Christ-centered marriage and one that is Christian-centered. It's likely that Mama had never been happy anyway and now was never happier to be miserable with our somewhat mutual decision to live in a tree. But she was braver than most in her position—just enough so to keep me from backing away from mine. The financial disaster hadn't made our marriage worse but instead had exposed it for what it truly was—very Christian-centered. I took care of the yard and the gnomes; she took care of the tree. *Abba* would have to take care of us both, without any more help from me.

RECONSIDERING THE LILIES

In between looking for work and working odd jobs, ferreting through court dates and harboring concerns over our original home, now an upside-down rental with tenants angry about those leaks and creaks we left behind in the night, I busied about the backyard and anywhere else beyond the sound of deliveries, door knocks, and dumb phone calls. Either corralling the thousand and one decorations behind the house or sitting in my car, often still in the garage with my key in the ignition and not enough gas to circle the block, I sulked, and shouted obscenities, and still managed to praise the One who'd allowed it all to happen.

If God was going to squeeze this out of me, He'd have to do it in the privacy of my own padded cell, a one-car hangar that smelled of bearing grease and patched tires, a room where

I could scream without being heard and hate myself out loud. *"God, if You're going to teach me a lesson ... do it here and hurry up. Take my hammer now and beat me into something my wife can be proud of."* It was a ceremony I continued for an entire season without a whisper from heaven in return.

A SENTIMENTAL COUNTERFEIT

Journal Entry #11

If God and His creation are the real match made in heaven, then marriage is an astonishing composite designed to depict and apprehend that very substance. It is the soil at ground zero where the seeds of life, love, and intimacy with God take root on earth in preparation for eternity with Him. Yet simmering just beneath is the potential to painfully miscalculate God's intention and head in the opposite direction.

Even after years of matrimonial refinement and reflection, I was unclear about the main thing: A Christ-centered marriage is an original and priceless work of God, and a Christian-centered marriage is nothing but a cheap knockoff.

With an identity based on earning power and accomplishment, I measured leadership by how well I used those abilities to satisfy the needs of my family, particularly those of my spouse. The more I could offer her by hard work and sacrifice, the more pleasing to her I became, and the better leader I would ultimately become. As a committed Christian, I viewed it simply as the common sense of loving my wife as Christ loves the church.

It has a nice ring because by all practical appearances, working diligently to offer her the best was genuinely carrying out the command to love sacrificially. It's a subtle misdirection that is a bit more obvious in written form but in the course of daily life becomes clouded by our equally subtle strongholds (inflexible, misguided perceptions), and defaults unintentionally to a form of idolatry—one that, ultimately, neither spouse can detect.

In other words, I was more willing to have my efforts tested and approved by my wife than to have my faith tested and found pleasing to God. As a result, my affection for Him was inadvertently smothered by my affection for His best creation. When I lost the ability to sacrificially provide, my noble paradigm of leadership in the home was exposed as a sentimental counterfeit.

Even then, my immediate reaction was one of logic that says with great confidence, "Sacrificing for our family *is* pleasing to God." And I read book after book that basically agreed, and provided me with long to-do lists on how to be a better spouse by doing more, giving more, and giving up more of myself.

But it would take looking below the surface of that sacrificial sentiment to see the war of principalities where an enemy is hard at work manipulating truth in order to unseat God as my absolute "seek first" focus, where "all these things," such as a good marriage, are added anyway. And where becoming a leader in the home is as simple as literally taking God at His word and walking by faith instead of by the seven steps of godly self-improvement.

It was an adjustment for me that ultimately came by hammer, chisel, and shop vac as my duty-bound, hardwood commitment was chipped at, flung down, and sucked away from a dirty garage floor. I suppose that a silent God is the villain for any man with clogged ears and bad eyesight, but in the end an irresistible hero for a worn-out fool.

AMAZINGLY ODD GRACE

After weeks of cleaning the yard, reading marriage books in my car, and complaining to God without regard to what His silence might be saying, I began to fall asleep without realizing it, several times a day. I would often be awakened by startling dreams and piecemeal pictures of things too weird to describe, but frequent enough to connect, like the phrases of good narration through a bad connection. Sometimes they came in the form of questions, like Bill Gates calling at 4:00 a.m. to ask if I'd like to be mentored by him at this time each morning. Or Bill as an infant screaming through the phone for someone much bigger to feed him. It was either temporary insanity on my part or the cinematic sport of God daring to speak to a man without ears or challenge the perspective of a man without eyes.

These two particular dreams occurred together over a twenty-four-hour period. Within that time God also reminded me of a lesson I learned as a child—one that always seemed clever, but would only become a spiritual revelation in the context of my current frustration.

In an instant of terrible misfortune, the details of which still make me cringe, one of my favorite childhood friends lost all sight in his right eye by the tender age of ten. With better than average vision, his left eye fully adapted and life was good in the end, but with a slightly different perspective.

We became pals through sports a year or so after his accident, and I never had a clue until he shared his thoughts about the experience. I found the entire idea intriguing, but for the longest time I considered he might only be playing a joke—how could a blind boy beat a two-eyed hotshot in basketball, unless of course, the hotshot was not so hot, or maybe just a gullible dope. But ultimately, it was blind-boy-Supermom who came to his rescue with proof that his story was true. I'd been beaten indeed by a kid with a lopsided view, and a sensitive parent who made darn sure that I knew.

As an inquisitive kid, I thoroughly enjoyed the suspense of not knowing if my friend was actually blind. The anticipation of finding out such a thing without being told was my curious delight at that age. But thanks to Supermom, I had to come up with a new source for entertainment, and I set out instead to find out for myself what being blind is really like—a science project of sorts where all the fun is asking the questions, *How did it feel to close the good eye? How could he keep his balance? Was it darker on the blind side?* I provoked, stroked, and constantly begged for better explanations, but the answers came, always the same, by him waving a hand in front of his eye and confirming to me that he *just couldn't see.*

It was clearly time for new tactics, such as a blue-ribbon, blind-man impersonation to try it out myself. So groping about the kitchen, I reached for his sassy mom's umbrella and tapped it back and forth along the linoleum, whacking their appliances, plastic chairs, and stucco walls. And with the sweetest of eyelid squeezes, I insisted impolitely that pretending was helping me relate.

Sick of it all, he looked at me with at least the potential of both eyes and said, "Kevin ... you're an idiot."

To which I responded, "Can't you see from the good eye

that I'm blind as a bat?" — never realizing how accurate my words were.

He fired back sarcastically, "Yep, that's it. The close-your-eyes-and-imagine-you're-blind thing. Stupid. Stupid and wrong. It's not like closing your eyes, wearing blindfolds, visiting caves, or any of that crap. When you close a perfectly good set of eyes, you don't stop seeing, even if you close them as tightly as you can and blindfold them ten times."

"No way, man!" I responded confidently. "It's pitch-black in a cave!"

"Okay, stupid," he said. "Then think of it like this. If you had no eyes, what would you see? Or better yet, try watching a movie with your kneecaps and then describe to me what you've seen."

Presto! It was a good word from the mouth of a boy genius, one who could fully comprehend blindness without being fully blind. It was also a lesson I would never forget, but one I had never applied to spiritual eyes until I could begin to see both sides of the problem. I suppose that God's amazing grace includes a window seat from space.

NOW I SEE

We often miss the truth because we're looking toward heaven (from earth) with "eyes to see" instead of looking toward earth (from heaven) and actually "seeing" by the Spirit of God who dwells within us. Perhaps the bottom line, for at least some of the spiritually blind, is that God uses crazy dreams to remove the *beams* from our eyes at just the right time — while we're still buzzing around the periphery, nobly attempting to tweeze our own specks with a little *Christian-self-help*.

As a faithful provider, I focused for years on how to please my wife, but in defeat I began to focus more on how to fix myself, believing that by doing so, I might somehow continue to please her through a new type of sacrifice. It all sounded good, and I learned some really good things about how men and women are different, with different languages and maybe even from different planets. But no matter how good the seven steps were or how many fine ideas I absorbed, the end result was the same, and ultimately left me with a nagging question: "Is any of this truly working?"

Upending my earthly perspective, however, required the unearthing of my sentiment—an identity still stuck in rational thinking with a "seek first the kingdom of your spouse" mindset, which meant that God would have to speak to a man with ears to hear and eyes to see, but one who remained deaf and blind by the common rationale of Christian culture. Appropriately, getting my attention called for course corrections that were idiosyncratic and corporately ridiculous, such as Bill Gates showing up in a dream to ask me a question. They were personal challenges to my faith as delicate as the weight of a fingerprint, yet as powerful as its billion-to-one distinctiveness. And therefore nearly impossible to ignore or rationalize in the way that I'd always done with Scripture.

For this reason alone, I began to pay attention as dreams became a kind of back door for me where God could sneak in behind my "yeah, but" logic and upend every accidental idol and Christian-centered sentiment, including that of self-preservation, so that by faith in Him alone, I could hear, see, and understand the literal truth of Matthew 6:33. "But seek first his kingdom and his righteousness, and all these things will be given to you as well."

Bill Gates or Jesus—which one would I take the time to be personally mentored by? Answering properly instead of honestly was a real temptation. It's a foolish comparison for a Christian, but one that illustrates how willing I had been to make time for the heroes of the world and not for the God who made them—the same One who feeds them all, including baby Gates. We all know that Bill never makes that call, but now I know that the One who made Bill calls every day, and I was just letting the phone ring.

So God was beginning to blur the landscape around me by turning my focus toward Him, softening the sharpness of logical ideas that I'd always known as mainstream Christianity—ideas that tug at us from the periphery of absolute surrender toward self-improvement by commitment to becoming a better believer. It was a landscape of skin-deep faith that flinches from the fires of suffering and opts instead for the cooler edges of safer, more practical thinking—and one where removing the beam before considering the speck is more about fixing oneself than facing our own hypocrisy.

If God only helps those who first help themselves, then His words are as common as those spoken by the heroes of self-help—easy to ingest, digest, pass, and forget. Casual hypocrisy may just be the most brilliant form of ignorance—glory to me by accident, where good deeds save souls, good ideas save marriages, and God's strength is perfected in my completeness.

Where, then, is the marriage capable of defying this kind of cultural gravity? In a humid little home, with moving gnomes and a couch wedged between the walls—a home that looked like a prison to a Christian-centered knockoff, but one that eventually became a palace for the Christ-centered original.

Journal Entry #12

The God who never sleeps and knows the number of hairs on my head watches over me as a father admiring his slumbering child. He waits eagerly for me while I sleep, to wake up and spend time with Him. But with only minutes to spare and a teenlike half-smile, I head past Him on the way to the hot shower, clean clothes, and coffee. I wonder aloud if any friends have a copy to lend of that great new book — the one on living a better Christian-centered life.

CHAPTER 9

SURRENDER

GOD LIKES PLAID

On the good faith of an older lady with little means, we settled reluctantly into the wee home Holly dubbed an "ugly plaid shirt two sizes too small" that God had insisted she wear for the rest of her natural life. A lady wrestler she became, with the brass to body slam angels and dog cuss any heavenly beings that rattled her scheme for a better costume—preferably a prettier shirt that fit.

We hunted for a month before that nasty little offer but she dodged it for a week after, finding two she "knew" were a better fit—including one we were "destined" to have that fell through an hour before signing the lease. Apparently God likes plaid and tiny abodes with perpetually broken air units. It was perfect for us, and she hated it. I hated it too. Especially when we had to decide between keeping a promise to pay the sweet landlord and keeping ourselves fed.

Thin and beautifully wrinkled, she had a countenance that mothered anyone close by with a firm hug and a handful of candy. She was delightfully frail and neat, with a spark of anticipation that strengthens her surroundings, ten feet deep. She moved us about the property with tiny hands painting pictures, pointing out the delicate features of her widow's nest, equally proud of the house and the spirit of life that made it a home.

It was clean in a cluttered sort of way, but cramped so close to the widow's godliness that we knew it was ours right away—a gentle rebuke for bad behavior, perhaps. It was like knowing one's miserable test score before the teacher ever hands it back. Our life was already full of red ink, and seeing up front that it would be impossible to pay the rent only made it look redder.

Our reservation didn't go unnoticed by this elderly dove, who decided without hesitation to take us both directly beneath her wing. Clasping the tops of our hands with hers, leaving just a trace of lotion, she bowed with a pause, then delivered a most unconventional notion.

I was expecting the "what happens if you don't pay" speech. But instead of a strong-arm, she prayed a strong prayer and confirmed out loud that the place was ours without any need to question. We each had different reasons to reject the opportunity, but honestly, there was nowhere else to go. With a pocket full of empty mint wrappers and the sense God gave a mule, I gambled once again on an idiotic plan to sign a lease I'd never be able to pay. One week later, about all the time we had left, we began walking by faith afresh—more foolishness it seemed than ever, but this time led by a different reward and ideas that were far less clever.

Another quick stroke of the pen, and we hillbillies of Wild Elm were funneling in like wildlife to that tiny den at the end of Tree Trunk Drive. We were all five crammed in, cuddled together like cackling hens with no room to spread their wings. The movers had become old friends—people we see about once a year for cold drinks, small talk, and gawking at each other's less appealing lives, like a blue-collar cocktail party three years running. We had hoisted loads of high-quality furniture and dumb things made by sweaty people in faraway places, twice on the way up the mountain, and now with a little help from gravity, and one-tenth the stuff, back down to the ground for a long-term roll in the mud—hillbilly-style.

Our new surroundings were adequate, but required several weeks to become accustomed to. The stores and parks could be reached on foot, but the traffic noise was nice enough to meet us in our own backyard—a yard these maiden tenants had vowed to improve by breaking a few of the rules.

"Folks, all I ask is that you maintain the lawn," our sweet landlord had said, "and if you'd like to paint, just keep the walls neutral."

I heard "leave the yard as is," but my first job, according to Holly, was purging the grounds of all knickknacks, scalloped bricks, trinkets, and chimes. Pluck, load, and wheel those lovelies away—some into piles for redistribution later, others shot like wads of paper in or at the waste can to never be seen or heard from again. It was a good plan, I suppose, to unclad the plaid and make it all feel a tiny bit bigger. Holly's self-appointed task was liberating the walls of the first lady's best with splashes of fresh yellow paint—a good start, according to Holly, in our noisier, sardine-can-sized, bearable new life.

My concern was rent, taking care of the sweet soul who

had so graciously taken care of us without gasping over our dilemma—a decision made not by sympathy but leadership, good Samaritan-style. So for me, the bottom line was to pay her in full and always on time, no matter what it took. Pride perhaps, or determination, with a pinch of Robin Hood nobility that reminded me she wasn't a bank or large corporation but indeed a true friend with her own promises to keep. It would be something I could wear on my sleeve and look at from time to time to remind me that I had a part to play in helping God play His. Or so I thought.

CAUGHT BETWEEN TWO KINDS OF FOOLISHNESS

Setting up base camp on a wink from heaven is one thing, crossing the mountainlike months ahead is another. My new sense of earnest, no longer aimed at grand accomplishment, was not quite ready to follow the lead of a God who needs no advice. God may have done it for us the first time, but I had to do it for Him the next fifty. I was looking out instead of up, running too far ahead without being led, countering with *yeah, buts*, and the holy grail of convention known by most as common sense.

Lo and behold, and long before any moment of panic would arrive, the panic began on the inside as I was desperately caught between two kinds of foolishness—living like there is no God and talking like there's nothing else that matters. I began desperately looking for ways to make those payments from Day One—silly ways that accomplished nothing but shallow prayers, one-sided conversations, and something I didn't appreciate until later—my own little version of Psalms that I call a journal.

Journal Entry #13

There is a point in every gamble where the willing fool has a malignant form of hope. A moment of exhilaration presoaked in flammable remorse. Thank you, God, for opening this door. Please don't slam it on my fingers. The attitude of exuberant prayers and maniacal nail-biting until the horse nears the finish line three lengths behind. Those seconds before a certain loss when we see that God has a plan and it's not as good as we thought. A kind of pre-defeat by logic, reduced to emotion and made fact by the will, a torn-up bet ticket before the race goes still.

Between all the falling asleep, forwarding of résumés, and looking for God in the mirror, I worked like a fiend behind the scenes to become a web genius and work-at-home entrepreneur. Hoping to surprise my plaid-clad wife with a wad of cash to add to our stash, I signed up for a hundred and one schemes, surveys, and shopping sprees and gambled my time on a new kind of slot machine. Advertising gimmicks that promised income by the penny for only minutes of work. Surveys about everything from soft drinks to fabric softener, which took anywhere from fifteen minutes to an hour — a piece of my time on earth I'd like to exchange for a month of staring at the ceiling. Half of them led to scams, the other half to online credit for the very same products I reviewed — shipping not included. The only return, in fact, was an email address in ruins and a lesson learned that would make a less desperate fool turn back.

BEGINNING TO SWEAT

We'd managed to scrape by for the first two months with odd jobs and odd solutions, such as garage sales and selling small things—leftovers from a previous life: TVs, tools, paraphernalia for patios, outfits, knickknacks, and remaining jewelry, nearly all of which was used to pay rent. But the third month, when it was devastatingly humid inside and outside, I found myself with nothing to show but a fistful of change, nothing left to sell, and a dry spell from any kind of work that made money.

I was left with a tilted sense of awareness that God indeed is good, but apparently not good enough. We just felt sick. Like discovering-there's-a-turd-in-the-birthday-cake sick. And my secret plan for extra cash made it all seem worse.

With nothing left for the upcoming rent payment, no income, and literally nowhere else to go, it appeared our lives would be turned upside down for the second time in months. Becoming homeless was once again a legitimate concern, and one that was growing with each passing week.

In addition to that overwhelming issue, we had a less threatening but more immediate one to deal with. During the first week of that month, still pecking away at surveys—something no doubt reserved for the tenants of hell—my own little corner of workspace was feeling just as hot. Slightly confused by those first few beads of indoor sweat, I thumped in frustration at an aging thermostat. It was eighty-five and climbing, and for the next half hour I paid my final respects to an A/C unit I'd barely gotten to know—as it gave out in a chorus of screeches and halts, and stayed out for nearly a month.

A GOOD WAY TO DODGE THE RENT

Springtime repairmen become summertime saviors from the wet heat that makes your hair follicles forget their inhibitions and abandon themselves to the humidity, like sweat-soaked groupies. We were no exception, as each day it became ten degrees hotter in the house than on the outside—something my wife despised, along with timid deodorant and a plaid shirt meant to be worn by a mid-seventies fifth grader.

Two small fans splitting time between the bedrooms left us with no funds for the more robust model needed to cool down the living room and kitchen. On the bright side of things, a little heat was fine for the moment, as sweating profusely helps purge the body's impurities. It was almost like working out by sitting still, so it was not a big deal for a day or two. And with such a kind friend to call, one we could barely address as landlord, there was apparently no cause for concern. On the other hand, with the all-business version that answered, maybe we should've been concerned just a little, as our favorite dove of a landlord had put on a business suit and gone looking for a deal.

Our first repair encounter was with a cut-rate shop that sent two guys in a rusty van with a ladder on top—and, more importantly, stenciled on its side were the words "Not When It's Absolutely Broke—A/C Repair." Or so it seemed. They stayed for an hour and tried to explain the situation with gestures and broken English. *It can't be fixed*, I'm sure was the intended message—the wrong message, I supposed. Still a landlord myself, ironically, I understood the need to get several opinions. But after several days without a word from our friend, I knew the ordeal was far from over.

The next chap was a one-man show with more incoming

phone calls than tools. A Tinseltown type, complete with indoor shades, an autograph pad, and a three-day wait for house calls — a repair guy for the stars possibly. So three more days of blistering heat had won us a half-hour visit with the Elvis of A/C repairmen — ten minutes spent on the problem, and twenty spent answering disco-tech ringtones or texting another repairman. Yet by some miracle or new form of A/C CPR, he was able to fully revive that poor beast, just long enough to smile wickedly and head back to Hollywood. Thanks a million, Dr. Cool. We were back in business — for about an hour.

Rejoicing, we had currents of mechanized air teasing hands and faces like dirty kids knee-deep in fire hydrant rapids, cool air that felt better than a one-hour shower on a one-week layer of stink. But the hour passed, the unit breathed its last, and our hope in mechanical miracles had fallen victim to the torment of tenant protocol. "We need Elvis back here immediately." I phoned in the bad news right away. Lady Bird in pinstripes passed it on sometime later. But the one-man show from nowhere had packed and left the building for at least another three days. Her sweet apologies dripped from the answering machine that evening, but evaporated quickly into a thousand-pound cloud of frustrated humidity.

Several days later, he reappeared for an encore performance of Swagger Live at Tree Trunk Drive — now a vacation spot on the equator. With every window and door flung wide open, I walked him in with a word of caution. "Let's get the problem resolved today and worry a bit less about the symptoms. Thanks in advance." With a hellish suck, the attic took him prisoner for an entire hour of clanks, clunks, and curse words, all dropping pleasantly from the mouth of my ceiling. Up and down he climbed until he stayed down, like a worn piston, shirt four shades darker and dark shades bent out of shape, barely hanging from his collar.

"Truth is," he said, "she needs to replace the unit."

This went on for two more weeks until everyone, reputable or not, agreed that, as desperate as we might be, there was no way to repair what must be replaced—a great source of consternation for a precious friend with the means to fix the machine, but not enough for a new one. I understood completely, but then again I couldn't. In a climate where ugly things grow best, my anger had grown legs and dashed off with the rest of my perspective. The hotter and slower the circumstance, the faster my anger ran toward relief—so fast, eventually, that even my best intentions were short of breath and spinning at the speed of my incredible selfishness—which is precisely when it all began to make sense.

Our situation provided a fantastic excuse for dodging the upcoming rent—bingo! This was God's way of meeting our need—payment by suffering indeed, through a month of deep-South humidity and no air—air we paid for with jewelry, but never received. All things considered—with rent due the following week and nothing left to hock—why not? Although life was pretty rough with our in-house climate, if we couldn't pay the rent, considering where we might end up made it a lot rougher. With a little help from a broken A/C unit, prolonging our discomfort might buy us another month of freedom and temporarily save us from something much worse. *Thank You, God, for the victory of faith!* At least that's how I rationalized it for a little while.

MUMBO JUMBO GUMBO

I realized very early in our financial crisis that I couldn't dig myself out—that I couldn't fix everything by grabbing my own bootstraps. After reading about the faith of George Müller—a man who believed it was normal to rely on God alone—my heart was decidedly ready to attempt a life of absolute faith. However, by the end of three short months in a plaid-clad tree trunk, I was living by something different—a combination of logic, gut-wrenching emotion, and strong-willed desire— which I proudly still referred to as faith.

But as God tested me with tougher assignments, I began to silently reconsider the definition of faith with a hypocritical slant.

Maybe I'm not "the provider," but standing by while my family is in danger of losing their home for the second time is taking the idea too far!

Surely God helps those who at least try—I thought.

It's just who I am—I began to believe all over again.

I have to do something other than just pray—I determined.

But it was Mumbo Jumbo Gumbo! What a mess and what a worldly fool was I. Two steps forward, three steps back, trusting God by trusting myself, sitting still by moving, listening by giving Him advice, and consequently failing in dramatic fashion. And completely overlooking the truth that anything other than prayer—unless led by the One I'm praying to—was still using my own strength. Maybe the fact that my absolute hypocrisy would pay nothing but hypocritical dividends was God's way of penetrating my soul (mind, will, and emotions) in a new way. So that I would eventually learn it would take more than a heart filled with desire to actually "live" by faith.

Journal Entry #14

What in the world would cause two blind bats to partner up and chase down the local hippie humanitarian, but faith — or so I thought. I can see it vividly, arms in the air, groping around, running into each other — blind men running after and calling for help from the One Guy with all the answers. The picture alone might be considered a comedy sketch, but the truth behind it is as serious as a wasted life. "Have mercy on us!" Desire, determination, desperation are met with a question: "Do you believe that I am able to do this?" At which point I pause to say, "Pardon me, sir, but why in the heck do You think I'm tripping over myself to get to You?" To which He might respond, "Well, I can see your desire to be healed, but what I really want to know is, Do you have faith? There is a difference."

THE GOOD NEWS

The news came from our landlord about three days before the end of the month. "Thanks so much for your patience," she said, "but I have some really good news! I've been praying about this issue for weeks and wasn't sure what to do. It was all so unexpected, really, and quite a bit more than I could afford. But I'm so happy to tell you that a unit the size of an iceberg has been provided by the Lord. So hang in there just a few more days, my patient friend, and we'll bring this mutual inconvenience to a much-welcomed end."

With a fistful of faith and one full of candy, our crafty little friend had managed to sweet-talk God, or someone not as shrewd, into sending us a brand-new unit on the day our rent was due. I should have been happy, but any relief that I felt about receiving a new A/C unit was quickly overshadowed by the looming potential of our becoming homeless in a matter of weeks.

My only recourse, as mentioned, was to demand from our landlord a rent-free month in exchange for the one we'd just spent in plaid-shirt hell. From my point of view, the fact that our unhealthy environment — household temperatures that exceeded one hundred degrees — was a prolonged and continuing issue completely justified that demand.

As a landlord myself, I wondered how any decent colleague could accept payment when his or her tenants are forced outdoors to find relief. It was as if we'd been living in a tent, for goodness' sake! So as long as this burden continued, I believed we had a fighting chance to keep a roof over our heads, at least for another month — all for the cost of a little more sweat.

It was by this rationale that a "good news" call from our landlord *before* the rent came due was cause for great concern, as it would establish a "let's all put it all behind us" effect and leave me with little or no leverage. But in spite of the call, with seventy-two hours to consider it all, I continued my plan of attack.

Yet sometime during those blistering hours, and somewhere between my "rights" and doing what is right, truth nibbled away at my posture from the inside, like a swarm of stealthy termites. And I made a better decision — *simply trust God!* Ultimately, it wasn't the iceberg that sank my position, but the holes in my leaky character, thought worthy by its valiant ability to stay afloat, but only truly made worthy by having the integrity to just let it sink.

True surrender was not an end to be navigated by what I might say or by what I might do, but rather a condition that allows God to reveal the difference, then reconcile the two by whatever means He chooses, come what may.

On the day the new A/C unit arrived, my wife and I were relieved to know that at least our house would be cool, and somewhat inspired that we might all complain a bit less, not only about the heat but about the confines of sharing such tight spaces. Surely the little plaid tree felt roomier at thirty degrees below melt. Unless, of course, we'd be moving again to something much larger, more affordable, and perhaps even something without a roof, such as the park or grocery store alley nearby. But that was entirely up to God, I had finally, and somewhat begrudgingly, concluded.

The unit arrived with a team of specialists, well-groomed, tooled up, and huddled behind the door, tapping their watches and knocking politely.

But before my wife could answer, the phone rang a serious ring and pulled her in the opposite direction.

"Just let it ring," was my response.

"Just get the door," was hers.

Neither of us liked the odds. But after peeking through the window, I was glad to do the honors, and she was glad to hang up quickly if necessary. I suppose we were both due for a dose of raised expectations — especially me.

I answered the door expecting a backhanded blessing, a half-eaten treat, a plane-crash-in-waiting with an air-conditioned seat. She answered the phone with a better opinion of God and actually heard from Him. Amazingly, without one mention of our need, we had received an anonymous donation, a check made out to me for just enough — exactly enough — to pay for another month in the tree, now a cooler, more spacious, long-term destination with a little less baggage and a much safer landing.

JUMP

Years back, my best friend and I decided to give skydiving a try—at least once. Actually, he decided, and I went along for the ride, feigning agreement in hopes that we'd never arrive, having mocked the idea many times before. Even if we did, I'd be happily unable to cover the cost of admission. We both had a taste for adventure, as well as a good dare, mostly from a mutually insatiable curiosity. In fact, we made the drive in a car without an ounce of gas to spare and a lawn chair on the passenger side. But unlike my friend, my curiosity never included skydiving, mountain climbing, or anything that required being more than a few feet from the ground. So on this occasion, knowing the cost ahead of time, I was perfectly content to be secretly broke. Unfortunately for me, however, that was something he'd already considered, and covered, supposing it was better to die together, and leaving me fresh out of excuses.

The training, referred to as "jump school," was an episode of spare-part lunacy—a one-hour video as old as the Korean War, two apathetic leaps from a three-foot platform, and a guy named "Lucky" for an instructor. The aircraft was basic, smaller than I'd expected, with a cabin roughly ten feet square, completely bare minus the metal tread plate that lined the floor. There were no seats, except for the pilot's chair that could hardly contain the hooligan assigned to our flight—a pilot, I think—a pirate, I know, who looked and acted like the aviation version of Blackbeard's ghost. I suppose we were too dumb to be hopeless at this point.

The flight was short and serious, filled with "we got 'em now" radio talk. My friend jumped first after reaching the drop zone, leaving me alone with this maniac, a man twice my size with a menacing laugh and a hurry-it-up glare. Along with some words of encouragement—"You ready to die, boy?"—I was pretty sure I needed to go before he extended a leg and forced the issue.

So with both eyes and one big toe inching through the hole where a door should've been, I stared at the ribbons and rectangle patches three thousand feet below, gutless, scared, still deciding. More encouragement. "That'd be the ground, boy, exactly where you're going, one way or another."

Hypnotized by flashes of a fat pirate pushing me out and the pride of actually being out, I stepped fully onto the wing-shaped gangplank. There I froze, waiting for just the right moment, with a Superman grip, considering, considering, thinking. The plane was crawling at about ninety miles per hour to avoid overshooting the target, a fleeting target for a seasoned pilot with a slug on his wing. And well before I planned to jump, I jumped, startled by the loudest muffled word I'd ever heard: "Arch!" That was the green-light word from the pilot, who was basically saying, "Go now or you'll end up in the electric wires."

I was a novice, so my chute was attached to a static line—a long tether connected inside the cabin that automatically pulls the rip cord after a few seconds of free fall. A good arched posture reduces the likelihood of getting strangled; a bad one doesn't. My fall went from awkward to ugly to inside out as I got tangled in momentary slack that pulled off an arm—at least that's how it felt.

Far worse, the interruption caused the parachute to deploy but fail to open, which meant that I was falling, not floating. It was as if I'd been attached to an airless balloon and tossed off a building. Somehow I'd gone from my best friend's car on a lawn chair to being a bag of sand in midair, with nothing but big blue sky and a bit of unruly nylon to keep me company. The aircraft disappeared into the clouds.

Journal Entry #15

Gazing through the open door of an in-flight aircraft, frozen by the sight of the ground thousands of feet below—the next few steps depend on whether or not we trust that thin strip of fabric attached to us, the one that will never fully open if we don't fully jump. Unpack it, repack it, jiggle the cord, look at it three times, and twiddle it four, but a parachute simply won't work unless it's fastened to a fall. It requires the force generated by actually falling to push open the canopy—the death plunge to transform it into a life-saving plane of resistance. Through faith that death plunge becomes a controlled fall, slow and easy, delivering us safely to our destination—good ground. The high ground of intimacy with God, the only place we stand tall enough to reach our kingdom potential.

A parachute doesn't open until you jump. Mine finally did and ours was just beginning to. We lived in that heat for nearly a month, in spite of all the comforting words from our aging landlord, and learned a valuable lesson. Not how to appreciate our surroundings, but how to view God affectionately as a truly good Father we can rest in.

He continued to provide in unexpected ways because providing is what He does, unexpectedly mostly because we'd forgotten the blessings of our past—miracles that are hung like portraits of long-gone descendants in the halls of our hearts, but with so many, we can't quite remember their names or their significance to our lives. But He was maturing us beyond the specific concerns of meeting new needs with old ways, pler, single expectation—a single affection.

Without knowing the how, or even holding on to the expectation that He would, we began to rest in the knowledge that He is good—that He really is good enough to simply do what's best. And we began to rest in the unvarnished belief that He is so generous, in fact, that He withholds long enough to stretch us, to grow our affections and desires for Him as a Father. As our season unfolded, our memories continued to fade but our good opinions of God multiplied.

THE SAFETY OF GOD'S VOICE

After nearly a year, the plaid shirt was still plaid, the tree trunk still dark and slightly waterlogged. Half-baked attempts to find professional work had served and failed as protection from the opinions of smarter people. We all raised a glass for a better year, and some made a toast to the lazier, luckier man I'd become. But I no longer cared. The internal struggle between having a determined commitment to live by faith and utterly surrendering to a good Father had come to an end. The testing, however, intensified.

In a moment of bootstrapping glory toward the end of our lease, I received a gift-wrapped surprise, a call from the local office of a very large corporation. I was offered a position in the field of my expertise, with no travel and a six-figure compensation package, including benefits. Halleluiah in the name of all that is practical, a high-end job, close by—one I could do with my hands tied behind my back. Though I had never applied, the company found my résumé on a job site. Apparently, my qualifications exceeded those of their entire pool of applicants, so the position was mine if I wanted it.

The interview was a formality, a brief discussion about duties, compensation, and the timing of my start date. They gave me a week to confirm, with a planned orientation the following week. The only knot left untied was a "yes, and thank you very much." My heart leapt at the prospect. With no income at all and a short supply of groceries, I rejoiced at such an overwhelming answer to our prayers. This was the answer everyone else had been waiting for.

As the week passed, I prepared with eager anticipation at the starting blocks of a new livelihood and crossing the finish line of this holy-crap-in-a-bucket lifestyle. During that time, something occurred that turned my newfound faith on its ear—an ear, allegedly, that was beginning to hear the sound of God's voice through dreams. By this time in my career as clown prince of fools and lucky sluggards, I slept very little. The nights were long and spent striving to make an income in the early months, and studying the Scriptures in the latter. And as I've mentioned, I made up for the lack of wee-hour slumber, unwillingly, throughout the day.

One such day, just after the interview, my tired mind landed on the carpet following a bit of journaling and sprawling for hours over the work material. With impeccable timing, I encountered the shortest worst/best dream I've ever had—one without color or cinematic flair, just the simple voice of a man who seemed to care little for my desperate need to sleep. In fact, the sound was startling enough to wake me up and wonder if I heard it aloud, like a prank being played from somewhere inside the room.

Here's what I heard with absolute clarity: *"I've provided the job to give you a choice between the safety of the world and the sound of My voice. Take it if you like, but before you do, know I've got something much better for you if you're willing to choose Me instead—though it will be hard."*

Astonishingly simple, incredibly intricate, a dilemma fit for a fool, a giant mess with an unknown blessing. I could either believe it was God's voice and make that choice, or completely reject it as a diabolical plot from the Enemy to keep us in poverty. But if it was God, I had an even greater impasse—freedom for my family, freedom from the skull-crushing vise of debt, relief from the piercing eyes of practical politics, a fresh coat of paint for my life, pantries full of groceries, utilities paid in advance, and heroic applause for grabbing my own bootstraps and getting on with my former life.

Or I could accept my Father's invitation to a lifestyle of endurance, ridicule, and hope against hope that eventually my vapored existence might reach its full potential, the "more" that nearly every believer is longing for but few ever seem to find. It's easy enough to dismiss for the "yeah, but" society and wiser majority, but given my recent history of dreams and peculiar confirmations, this was a predicament akin to dismantling an atomic bomb with no experience, or giving it a good *pshaw* and declaring by logic that it could only be a dud.

Well over a year had tinkered its way through the mechanics of my faith, months of undoing what most believed should be taped up, bolted down, and professionally repaired. God was teaching me to surrender, removing those worn-out, wedged-in parts piece by piece and replacing them with Himself. This was the culmination and moment of reckoning, a decision He was leaving to me alone, about Him alone—a decision between a pat on the back from His generous hand—a new engine for old ambitions—and a lifetime kiss on the face from His affection-ate lips, the keys to an unfathomable kingdom intention.

Our friendly landlord had only planned on leasing her home for the year and then selling. So with a one-week supply of groceries, a month away from moving, and still jobless, penni-less, and extraordinarily foolish, I declined the offer and walked away from a guaranteed six-figure income. "Give me the hard thing, Lord." Tired of being pushed around by what is seen, I jumped into a future of being led by what is unseen, hoping that once again the chute would open by the upward thrust of faith. I prayed for an entire day before sharing the dream with Holly. She agreed that this was a test of epic proportion, one that would once and for all demonstrate what it means to truly walk by faith—a lesson that God was willing to teach if I was willing to completely surrender. The time had come for me to do just that.

Within two weeks, God confirmed my decision through another unexpected phone call. A former client with a dire emergency was asking for my immediate assistance. The proj-ect had an impossible deadline attached to huge financial risks. Even with years of experience, it would require a miracle to accomplish. But for me, the call itself was the miracle—and miraculous confirmation that I'd made the right decision to trust God's voice.

By choosing Him over the safety of the world, God pro-vided me with two weeks of work with an income that would've required at least six months of fifty-hour weeks at the full-time position I had just declined. So I gladly accepted the challenge! And by God's grace, it was completed on time to provide an enormous financial benefit for the company. In return, I was paid enough for only two weeks' work to cover the needs of my family for the next six months. Arch! Canopy open! And a very safe landing for a guy who trusted God when he was completely broke. Praise God!

In the same month, our final few weeks in the land of yard gadgets and gnomes, our city suffered the worst flood in the last hundred years and was declared a federal disaster area by the U.S. government. Thousands of homes were destroyed, including many in our own neighborhood. Two in particular that were completely flooded were the same two homes we had attempted to rent, and came very close to renting, one year earlier. While we were heartbroken for those families, we couldn't help but be further humbled by God's amazing grace — a plaid shirt two sizes too small that probably saved our lives in more ways than we can ever imagine.

CHAPTER 10

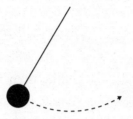

FAITH PENDULUM

ONE FINAL JOYRIDE

For a guy who once preferred a car that had a lawn chair for a seat and was thrilled to dumpster dive as a child when a friend's cupboard was bare, becoming a bona fide high-end auto thief as an adult wasn't beyond plausibility, if you would have asked my wife. Out for an evening to celebrate our twelfth anniversary, we dined and dashed off for a moonlight drive and pulled into an auto dealership. I'd always enjoyed window-shopping when least convenient.

"How romantic," she said. "A dark parking lot full of cars we can't afford."

"I'm sorry, but since we're here, would you mind if I got out for a quick look?"

"Suit yourself, but please hurry up."

Five minutes later, I pulled up, like a troubled convict, in a mint condition something-or-other with a sticker price just under the cost of a modest house. "Unbelievable! The doors were unlocked and the key's still in the ignition. Let's take it for a spin."

There's nothing quite like the rush of surprising her with a maroon slice of heaven, an SUV with leather seats and its own south London accent willing even to direct our escape from the dealership lot. Reluctantly, she hopped in for a joyride and hung in suspense for thirty seconds while we dusted our way out the back and onto a country road. Stealing a car for a momentary high, I suppose, is not much different from buying one I couldn't afford to feel like a momentary champ. She'd been eyeing this one for a year, but only mentioned it once. "Happy anniversary. It's all yours. Bought it last week just for you."

Those priceless few seconds in January 2008 lasted for two years. She loved it and I loved her, and neither of us had an inkling that we'd eventually have to let go of such a precious reminder of that moment. It was not just another vehicle. In fact, we all enjoyed it and held on much longer than we should have out of sentiment. Fortunately, the vehicle retained enough equity that even missing a few payments hadn't forced us to dump it on the same lot we'd found it. By the end of our plaid-shirt lease, however, we had to sell quickly to settle the debt before the lot came along and grabbed it.

Moving again meant further downsizing, not of material things, but the subtle burdens that kept us from becoming all that God intended. We had many new things to learn and unload just ahead—pride that befalls the sufferer, that twinge of moral superiority that sneaks around in the shadows of our own cross, and the misunderstanding that faith is a destination rather than a shield for the journey toward intimacy with God.

Our landlord was flexible enough to allow us two extra weeks to properly relocate, and with that window and a few months' income, we decided to steal one final joyride in Holly's anniversary gift. We had a future that for the first time in a year went several months deep, which was just enough time to open our eyes a bit wider and reconsider God's strategy—the why and aim of His goodness toward us, for the sake of our responsibility to steward it. Moving to a completely different city might be good start, so off we went to investigate.

Wadding up my life and starting over probably wasn't the answer, but after forty years it was a natural default. It was certainly a more romantic option than moving back to our original house, the one we still owned by the skin of our tenant, who was ironically ready to leave. It was also still the home with odd neighbors who might welcome us back by paying us back in not so neighborly ways. No way, Jose, scratch the thought with an SUV that balks at every U-turn and talks about nothing but changing the scenery.

ICE CREAM IN THE HOOD BY GPS

In a whirlwind week of new towns and thousands of things to consider as a family, conversations that began with "wow, that's nice" always ended with "it's too hot—can we stop for ice cream?" Somehow our serious search for a better life had been reduced to a "who gives a crap, let's just eat" summer vacation. Honestly, it felt so good to have gas money and a week to breathe that finding an ice cream stand at every stop seemed a much better investment of our time together than sweating over mysterious locations, affordable housing, and schools. Especially since we had an onboard version of Posh Spice to demand us in the right direction. Kids shouting "ice cream" at the GPS, and me following her perfectly articulated directions, made it all feel spontaneous — something we all needed, something our children probably deserved by then.

Apparently the nearest ice cream spot was a mile or two down the streets of a fragile neighborhood with dilapidated homes, some sprayed with graffiti. It was the hoodiest hood I'd ever seen selling ice cream, definitely not a place for snobs. But by the time we realized something was wrong, against my wife's good judgment, I decided to complete the mission, to know what in the GPS was going on. Two more nervous turns and three times clicking the locks, and we followed our onboard voice to the same wooden shack I'd seen in an episode of *Cops*.

Forget nobility, my wife wanted us to make a not-so-subtle retreat, but for me that required a quick pass to get a better look, just to be sure. Five seconds extra for a stealthy turnaround in the parking lot and we'd head back out. There it was, a fifties-style ranch with blue faded paint, complete with a hand-painted sign in what should've been the backyard, a hood cream stand for one and all brave enough to find it — including the local foot traffic that seemed as captivated by our expensive vehicle as I was by their local establishment.

"Can we please go now?" Holly asked.

I agreed, but was overcome by the desire to know more, to at least find out if the place was still open, and if so, why here. Maybe it was just a house that used to be an ice cream parlor. All the kids could see was a picture of a triple-dipped cone and a list of prices.

"Come on, Dad, it looks so good!"

But after a few seconds, my imagination — prostitutes,

pimps, weird concoctions made over coffee tables in the name of all things rotten — kept us from going any farther.

"Sorry, guys — Mom's right."

With a quick spin of the wheels, I nearly mowed down two unwelcoming residents, gents exchanging midday gifts in the same gravel lot ten feet behind the vehicle, now making cap-gun gestures at me over the interruption.

"Whoops-a-daisy, guys."

The only way to avoid confrontation was to scare them with confidence, so I just kept going in circles. Fortunately the narrow drive-through offered the best escape, since the main road sat thirty yards beyond it. I knew then that the smartest maneuver would be to proceed ahead boldly, as if we were serious patrons — Food Network – types perhaps, with an acquired taste for something authentic and dangerously better than average.

So we crept along toward the window that appeared from a distance to be painted shut and draped in rotting material. Maybe it was a bedroom shade or curtains that hadn't been lifted for decades. A tenth of a mile to go at half a mile an hour, slow enough to squeeze past the building, but fast enough to maintain our distance from the figures in the rearview mirror. There was nothing left to do but move on through and pray the front side drive was clear.

But seconds before reaching the window, a face popped up from behind the shade and gave us all a good scare. It was the face of a pepper-haired man, stuffed between a white paper hat and pixie-sized black bowtie. He appeared to be about six and a half feet tall.

A little shocked, but still planning on passing by, I pulled to within inches of the window when he propped it open with a stick and deadpan stared me into a complete stop. I could see behind him that this was not only an authentic ice cream joint but a rather nice one—spotless, almost angelic, well engineered with rows of buckets brimming with colorful treats.

I couldn't believe it, and apparently neither could he. Instead of asking for our order he demanded to know where we were from. Still noticing movement behind us, I rolled slightly past him and spoke as softly as possible. He just stood there with a look that spoke without words—a kind of *how did you get here?* and *why are you still here?* admiration.

The kids were busy with more important things, such as reviewing the nine thousand ice cream options and making edits from the backseat—until their mom had enough of the entire scene and abruptly intervened.

"Kevin, we'll just take three of those, and let's be on our way."

"Six dollars, please," he said.

He disappeared briefly. It's funny how kids order food from the back like they're cracking a secret code, but prepare for its arrival like overwhelmed disaster victims. Just as I motioned for them to put down their game, my oldest daughter motioned back toward the man and said casually, "He's got a gun."

It wasn't really an unusual choice of words from a child with a robust imagination and thick glasses.

"Awesome. How about clearing a path because the ice cream's on its way back."

"Look, Dad, really—on the side of his pants."

Just then he stretched out the window with a hand full of goodies and a hip full of "oh, my goodness." She was right, the ice cream man had a gun indeed—a .357 Magnum strapped on and ready for action.

I looked at him and then the gun and then at him and said, "Listen, man . . ." before my wife grabbed at my shirtsleeve.

"No, Kevin, please don't ask!" But he kept both eyes on the delicate distribution of our three sugar cones, stuffed to the point of cracking with frozen green mint the size of planets—a work of art for two bucks each.

"Listen, man, why do you have that thing?" It was a long dark snake in a holster and stood out about three or four inches from his bright white ice cream pants.

He looked up as if he were going to shoot me to shut me up for the good of the rest of us before answering with an even more serious question.

"You mean you don't have one?"

As he handed me change from a ten, I said, "No way, friend. We came for ice cream, not a gunfight."

He responded immediately by poking his paper-hatted head all the way out the window and glanced in both directions.

"Okay," he said, then pointed toward the front exit. "You go out that way as fast as you can, and I'll cover you all. Go on now—*hurry!*"

He was completely serious and pulled his gun to prove it. My foot hit the gas, and we squealed out of his backyard, right into traffic.

My wife was frustrated with me for asking the question, and I was frustrated over his answer. The GPS had been our best friend and worst enemy. I've never been back, but I will never forget the contrast between the world we lived in that we called survival, and the one he survived in that he called life. Hood Cream, ice cream served with a flinch and the protection of a .357 Magnum.

BACK TO WHERE OUR THINKING WENT WRONG

Maybe a little romance is what we needed — a moment to ponder greener grass with a pocket full of cash. Sometimes all it requires is the courting of our horizons to learn that the world is neither round nor flat, but concave like a funnel. The only way out is backward, downward, and straight through the middle of tough circumstances. The best option for relocation, whatever it may have been, certainly included staying away from lengthy learning curves and new frontiers with Magnum-wielding good-humor men. In fact, our former neighborhood, the one we left for a better life three years earlier, never had more appeal, despite the quirky neighbors. Interestingly, the house would soon be vacant, as our tenants were in the final stages of construction on a new home.

On the other hand, with a much higher monthly expense and no long-term income, moving back in would be a completely unsustainable option and, likely, a foolish decision. Renting a small apartment made more sense, except for the fact that we'd be stuck with a vacant property worth far less than we owed, falling fast into disrepair. Taking on new tenants would be impossible without raising the rates to noncompetitive levels. The obvious solution was to short sell the house or allow it to foreclose, a move that would seal our fate as renters for at least another decade. We had less than a week to decide.

Ultimately, by the summer of 2010, having enough income to last six months at Tree Trunk Drive or six months in a comparable dwelling meant we had enough for about four in a larger, more familiar home that by God's grace we actually still owned. The difference was significant, but far less compelling by that time than exercising our faith. Outwardly appearing to throw caution to the wind was for us a great opportunity to publically express our belief that God alone is the provider. And at the very least, it was an honest desire for intimacy with Him—a search for what He was really up to and what He truly wanted for us, apart from the opinions of others, including our own.

Faith comes by the hearing of the word, but only with rigorous testing will its measure increase. By that standard, we moved away from the tiny, humid home that He provided for a time to adjust our thoughts and back to where our thinking went wrong. Additionally, with a little extra help from the bank, our mortgage payments could potentially be reduced—which is exactly what happened weeks later when they gave us the thumbs-up for a trial loan modification. By learning how to surrender, we found the freedom to explore the "foolish" desires, the illogical whims that God had long since placed in our hearts. We also discovered how misunderstood faith, like anything else, can pendulum out of control.

AN INTIMATE REVIVAL

During this period, my beautiful wife became inspired to her own radical revival by the words of a passionate young provocateur—David Platt, author of *Radical*. She's always been a doer, and we'd both learned to embrace the salty idea that less is often better than more, but I've never seen her so engaged, so energized to get her feet moving and hands dirty for God. She had somehow concluded through this popular read that our lifestyle, even after losing our livelihood, was still the wealthy antithesis of discipleship.

Let the pendulum swing.

Realizing the depth of her concern, we immediately discussed the idea and its author-prescribed antidote, a biblically defined radical lifestyle. Within the next hour we'd wistfully ruminated through the vanity of wealth and dispatched our remaining meager possessions. We'd adopted a kid from every nation and hauled them with us to a place requiring mosquito nets.

As she spoke, I listened respectfully and thought of how much more faith it must take for the anchor to move the boat—she being the anchor, me being held steady and afloat by the miracles we'd already witnessed, miracles now over-shadowed by romantic images of my family in safari gear, miming "Jesus Loves Me" and handing out bowls of food. It looked like full steam ahead for the *African Queen*. Bogey and Bacall with Bibles, dirty faces, one set of clothes, and a scriptural call to sell all in the name of pure devotion—count me in.

Then something unexpected occurred. She asked me to read the book and give her my opinion—not an easy thing for one who hates looking at checkbooks, following rules, and reading anything that I'll probably disagree with. But as the leader of my family, I reluctantly agreed, and God began to speak to me about our bigger, better, slightly holier new plans.

Journal Entry #16

For my wife:

It seems that fragile faith swings on a pendulum between pride, like Peter's drawn sword, and reproof, like the crowing rooster shortly after. The harder we push it one way, the farther it swings back the other. A kind of perpetual motion for the uninstructed soul that allows it to briefly taste and then retreat, to search for something new without losing the comfort of the familiar.

We pendulum toward a dream like bobbing for an apple,

but if we miss, we pendulum away as if that apple were a cluster of sour grapes. If we dream too much, we forget who God is, but if we bask in reproof, we forget who He made us to be. It swings and returns, keeping the many individual bodies perpetually one big part.

Some say Jesus was a radical, but I prefer to call Him the standard. Perhaps we need to sell our remaining possessions, but I prefer to dedicate their use. Perhaps we need to be missionaries, but I prefer to love by encouraging my neighbor. If the antidote is becoming a radical, then let's become radically intimate with our God. Let us directly personify the beatitudes, one by one, before we indirectly mischaracterize their sum total.

Our job was never meant to become jury by perpetual motion but to learn instead to listen to the voice of the judge. Whether we're called to fight or be still, to stay or to go, only His hand is steady enough to stop the corporate swing and lead us individually in the right direction.

If discipleship is about following God, then it begins with our eyes on His word and ears pressed against His heart. Without both, even the best-laid plans of well-intentioned hands will only flutter about in mime. His word reveals that we're a body indeed — but known by Him individually, created to know His voice specifically and then to follow it courageously.

His voice reveals the personal expression that activates its many well-designed parts: for martyr and missionary; for the ones who encourage, create, and build; for the ones who contemplate, teach, and inspire; for the ones who heal and keep the peace; for the ones who cook, clean, and bake things; and for the ones who rule nations, as well as those who've been given material wealth.

A disciple is defined by the willingness to bare his own cross rather than by the material things held in his temporary stewardship. While it is clear that the rich young ruler needed revival, it is equally clear that another rich man, the one from Arimathea, was a revival. Better to become radically faithful to what God places on our hearts than cramming our hands radically into a one-size-fits-all glove.

We thank you, Mr. Chick-fil-A, for giving us thousands of jobs, great food, and a place to eat where Christ is celebrated. We salute you, Steven Curtis and Mary Beth Chapman, for great music and a heart for parents called to adopt when they can't afford it. And may God bless you, Rick Warren, for reminding us that life was meant to be uniquely productive and for setting an example in your own radical river of giving. Thank you all for being individually radical by listening before moving, by following God's voice instead of miming.

Indeed, the Western dream has been perverted, but God's dream is right on track in those who listen to Him radically. If my heart is torn-up over Africa, then I must go. If it has been raked over hot coals for broken marriages, I won't go to Africa. Let us read, my dear wife, and be inspired by the godly firebrands who challenge us all to let go and do more. But keep in mind that God speaks directly to you about you, just as a good father should. Let us corporately agree and be individually led.

LET THE PENDULUM BE STILL

"Kevin, I feel like an animal caught in a trap, and, honestly, I'm about ready to chew off my foot to escape" was how Holly described the feeling of having room to breathe yet nothing to do but linger—a new kind of prison for the not completely surrendered. Neither of us wanted to slouch on the floor of our larger home or putter around, pausing at every clock and calendar. Gridlock was over, and we were ready to move forward at the speed of our dwindling resources.

Four months of better surroundings surely meant get up and go. But for the One paying the bills, the One who'd impressed upon me to be still, over and over again, it meant stop talking, complaining, planning, thinking, and drinking the darn Kool-Aid of rational men. Waiting like a child with nothing to do is a more delicate skill to master than waiting like a responsible adult for something more to do. Reluctantly Holly settled down, and I settled into a time of intimacy with God—two months of peace after twenty-two months of struggling through the mud.

I turned around to look back at nearly two years of deep corkscrew tracks from heavy steps with stones on our backs and no direction. By painful tuition I learned what we were not, what God was not, and a few things in between that were not—that faith is neither destination, determination, nor hope enthroned, like precious stones on people, provision, or perceptions. That His word is not a thing to be reasoned with, lock-picked by sleight of hand or reckoned by the slightness of mortal logic, nor some linguistic feast easily dissected by the greasy little fingers of brilliant scholarship.

Two months to reflect as well on the ground beneath and that which lies just ahead, and to comprehend what we were gradually being taught—that God's prolonged silence is the only GPS that waits to instruct until we have ears to hear that stiller, smaller voice. That His generosity is found in the least likely place—in suffering just enough that we cast off every ambition to sit still foolishly and listen when there is no sound.

And that His word is the only thing bound that is utterly unbound. It is as simple as milk for the hungry infant and as satisfying as meat for the ravenous man. It is an upper room for the weary, and blankets for the shivering sick. It is a place of healing, regeneration, and the tip of where His personality begins. It is the open door for personal revelation where, for anyone who is willing, God is willing to descend. And ultimately, it is where believers can ascend to affectionate hope that we'll never again waste what God has done for us all on wanting anything more than Him.

Let the pendulum be still.

PART 3

THE GAMBLE

CHAPTER 11

REST

Journal Entry #17

I stopped winking at Jesus from across the room with concerns about my schedule and reluctantly agreed to rest in His labor as an honored guest at His table. Seated like Mary in the midst of a King to be served by the Word made flesh, but squirming like Martha with apprehension that disobedient hearts are revealed by hands at rest. Thank You, Lord, for the offer, but please pipe down, have a seat, and allow me to polish Your throne. Because You, kind sir, are the guest at my table, and I'd prefer that You just make Yourself at home.

WRESTLING WITH REST

Our temporary liberation from financial pressure seemed to be God's way of luring us into the deep end of faith. As the freedom from the scorching demands of due process, debts, and basic needs became a downpour of hopeful expectation, it also brought the death-door risk of drowning in contemplation. Having the chance to simply rest at Jesus' feet was hypnotically freeing, but the idea of doing nothing at all with a short supply of cash was cliff-hung with uncertainty, like the sensation of falling.

Clearly, this was a do-over that for me was overdue, a balled-up life waiting in line for a two-year shot at the waste can. But I had no earthly idea what to do next or what the "do" in do-over actually meant. So my struggle was similar to Holly's — not quite as radical, but equally intense.

What does it actually mean to rest? How long does one consider before contending, or capitulate before conspiring? It may have a lofty ring, but as far as I knew, few people are afforded such a serious opportunity. For most, the idea meant vacation, or taking a deep breath. For some it might mean moderation, meditation, or letting go of stress — anecdotal antidotes bound in brief moments, dips in the roller coaster perhaps, but nothing with an unresolved end. And nothing as scary as hanging around our house without a plan.

REST PREPARES OUR EARS TO HEAR

One of the small pleasures shoved aside for nearly two years was spending time with my wife — celebrating each other's company by actually leaving the house to sit down at a table set just for us. To be waited on without worrying if we had enough for a tip. To share secrets and laugh about interesting people, to decline a refill and maybe guess at the check amount for the simple pride of potentially getting it right.

Our favorite was a cheap date of tacos à la carte, iced tea, and no dessert — a ten-dollar, two-hour investment of time together and time away from the kids, an investment that on one occasion was a rock-bottom price for a life-altering event. Just as God granted me insight for Holly in her hunger to be radically obedient, He did the same for me through her, in my desire to understand the meaning of rest.

"Kevin, earlier today I had a crazy thought," she said. "Or only a memory I guess, but one that flashed brightly enough to leave an impression with me throughout the day. Not sure if you would remember a five-minute conversation we had about five years ago. But I was planting flowers by the front porch and you sat down beside me to talk. You were having thoughts about shutting down your business, persuasive thoughts — a kind of discernment, I think, that maybe God wanted you to go into ministry. Do you remember?"

I responded with a slow, continuing nod while searching her expression for a bit more perspective. As my doubts about the idea gradually returned, I offered up a subtle *hmm* to politely acknowledge and consider her question more deeply. After pausing a second or two longer, I spoke.

"That's interesting . . . I haven't thought about *that* for years."

She gave me a few more seconds before inching forward to say, "Well, Kevin, I believe God is reminding you today."

She was as serious now as I was back then. At the time I was exhausted after a hard-fought effort to rebuild a troubled business, and we were beginning to enjoy a season of great prosperity. But just as my income reached its zenith, I began having an intense desire to give up my business for a life in full-time ministry — and a potentially devastating decrease in income.

That conversation Holly was referring to was one that unfolded with my briefly describing my impractical desire to her. But with every heartfelt word uttered, the idea sounded more and more ridiculous until we both moved on quietly. As a result, we ignored the still, small voice now affectionately referred to as "The Nudge," until it eventually became "The Shove"—and, ultimately, the falling sensation I was currently experiencing.

It was five minutes of trivial outdoor conversation for her, and five minutes of heart-pounding expression for me, after months of contemplation muted by practical rationalization. With nothing even remotely discussed or a single suggestion since, that inconspicuous nudge remained to our untrained spiritual ears a mere nuance for the next five years.

So now repeating her conviction to remind me of mine, she explained in detail one final time how the thought flashed like a comet through her mind, unexpectedly and without condition. But it was her final remark that lingered.

"Maybe we both should have listened."

OBEDIENCE BEGINS BY LISTENING

Two lovely daughters, each with their own brand of surprise, met us at the back door that evening with unmerited enthusiasm. The oldest, thirteen at the time, had created from scratch a ten-pound pan of I-couldn't-tell-you-what: gluten-free, chocolate-soaked, and peanut-buttered to the point that it was not only delicious but thoughtfully labor intensive. My wife doesn't eat wheat and we're both a bit particular, something my daughter had painstakingly considered. And by completely aiming to please, she persevered to new heights of a prettier-on-the-spoon-than-in-the-pan victory. We cheered.

The real surprise came when our younger daughter, age twelve, who is jealously competitive, made no effort to share the stage—not even a leg from behind the curtain. Like most kids, she lives for Mom and Dad's spotlight, especially when her sister is standing front and center beneath it. Normally she masterfully attains equal billing with one stroll through the kitchen. But this time was different. We cut the cake and praised the chef, and nothing was said. *Surely she's up to something*, we thought. A couple of hugs later, we discovered that our in-house baker had still not cleaned her room, walked the dog, or taken a bath as requested.

On the other hand, the one who wouldn't lift a finger to help with our sweet surprise had indeed cleaned her room, walked the dog, and taken a bath as requested, which was initially met with several huffs and at least one traditional, preteen eye roll. Through experience we understood that sibling personalities come packaged in beautiful but contrasting varieties of gift wrap. More often than not, each one needs a little freedom of expression in the way their gifts are unwrapped. But at the end of the day, every dog needs a walk and every kid needs a bath. So in spite of our sweet distraction, it was obvious that only one of our children had been obedient, but not necessarily for the obvious reason.

EARLY INSTRUCTIONS ARRIVE

I believed that Holly had been moved by God's Spirit and was riveted by it. The interpretation, however, remained as mysterious to me in my position as it might otherwise seem obvious to those who are not foolish enough to turn down a six-figure offer when the cupboard is all but bare. So by foolish interpretation, this revelation was likely a reminder that ministry is only a word, and for me a clever way to escape the truth that sitting still was still the right thing to do—because it was getting harder to do.

But even from a practical point of view, I'd have to say no thanks. I lived in the Bible Belt, for goodness' sake, where every third person is apparently called into ministry and the other two into missions. With no vision, credentials, or long-term means, a onetime smoldering impracticality that I left unattended was nothing now but ashes blowing in a thousand directions—ashes that would eventually learn to settle.

Honestly, all I really wanted five years earlier was something pure, a life's work given to encouraging and inspiring without the hint or attachment of financial gain, without all the ox-muzzling caveats afforded by Scripture, modernized and set aside for the dreams of the ordained. Ministry by surrender, a collision course with logic, impossible without a more foolish kind of faith that abandons the soul as its master and is led mysteriously by the indwelled spirit—fire brewed to a rolling boil until the aroma of heaven rises like steam from its lifeless ashes.

We were clueless back then, and now nothing but clues were offered that either God wasn't through or I'd become ingeniously disobedient. I had the entire evening to myself with a rescued memory and, as far as I knew, a shortsighted view of weeks ahead with nothing to do but think about it. I fell asleep in a mix of contrition and lopsided conversation with God. No dreams, just enough rest to cheat my way back to being wide-awake—like coffee at 3:00 a.m. with a three-lump thought stirred in—a thought that was without a doubt from Him: *"Wake up faith."*

Maybe it was an answered prayer—"Wake up faith," but what faith? Whose faith? I wasn't sure but in the context of my dinner conversation with Holly, I believed that God was giving me a call to action—another glimpse of His unfailing intention for my life. If it was a call to wake up the faith of others, it would certainly have to begin by getting my own faith out of bed.

Refreshed and guilty by association, I glanced at my Bible and considered what an amazing treasure it is. I considered how so many people, just like me, do what I so often did. "Not now, God." It sat on the floor, a few feet away. We sat there together, like people in pews who mentally cringe before conceding to greet one another. Remorsefully, I bent down to scoop it up, and thought, "*Okay, God*," before placing it reverently in my lap. It was perfect. Exactly right. In fact the perfect height to set my notepad on top of and comfortably begin to write.

Journal Entry #18

Lord, remind me again about the Word that was made flesh ... Its breadth and dimension are unrestrained by the flattened landscape of paper and ink. Its jasper walls of everlasting truth cannot be overtaken by the temporary weeds that men call facts. No literary arrow dipped in the flames of contradiction can set fire to this living water or breach the iron gates of its context. Not even the giant void of black universe can block the radiance of one single verse — "let there be light" — from Pennsylvania to Mongolia. It's a lamp to our feet that now stretches from Amish nightstands to the glowing cell phones of shepherds in the Gobi Desert. Oh, how the word is alive and powerful, sharper than any two-edged sword. Yet we hold it captive, locked in the scabbard, by leaving it unread and marching on ahead. Convict me to a life of resting against it.

CHAPTER 12

WAKE UP MY FAITH

Journal Entry #19

Blurry through a passing school bus window, it first appeared on a winter's day in the woods beyond our bus stop—woods with no roads or trails and trees of all shapes huddled in protest over the slightest trespass. Lodged for weeks behind layers of leafless oaks was a faded red pickup ... and its driver. Visible through a filmy driver's side window were dirty strands of middle-aged hair and a figure that lay toxically stiff like a rolled and folded carpet. I was fourteen when I found a dead guy in the woods. "Oh, my God," was the first thing on my mind but the last thing in my heart. After a few minutes I began to wonder if he had a wallet—one with an ID, of course ... but a few bucks wouldn't hurt. Yes, I really considered it. But as our great God has great concern, He kept my hands far away from such a dastardly deed as robbing the dead. I called the police instead, but next time, who knew.

ITION FOR A WILLING FOOL

d of immaturity was overcome by the age of eighteen when I made a commitment to the God I'd always believed in, a repentant admission of guilt and a promise to honor Him dutifully from that moment forward. It was a decision that brought goose-bumped satisfaction to my soul and reconciliation to its split personality. I'd been redeemed by the blood and forgiven, freed to look ahead and away from the baggage of my past. Free to claim victory over the Enemy when he scurried across my thoughts, unrestrained at last, with all parts of my soul marching in the same direction. But it was direction by default, unfortunately, as I was either marching in place to avoid the spook of supernatural things or chained to the world by the weight of its gravity.

So it took fourteen years for me to encounter death, eighteen to be rescued from it, and twenty-five more to be brought to life—to wake up my faith. Regrettably, twenty-five years of being absolutely "committed" to God rather than "surrendered" to Him left my soul stranded in neutral and, subsequently, strangled by invisible strongholds. As a "committed" Christian, I relied completely on my own understanding (common sense) and my own strength (determination). As a result, I sought to think and determine my way through faith rather than follow the lead of God's Spirit. Which is the opposite of what we see demonstrated by the heroes of faith in Scripture, who were nearly always instructed to go against logic, conventional wisdom, and common sense.

Not only is God not bound by these things; He rarely uses them to move us forward. My failure to believe this kept me running in place for a generation, held hostage by the gravities of the soul, by the appetites of the mind, will, and emotions, where strongholds remain embedded like enemy land mines from a onetime occupation. Consequently, my decisions were made by subtle compromises with logic, desires, and feelings, exalting human reason above the foolish things revealed to us by the Spirit of God. These compromises became misunderstandings, crystallized by compartment-like cubes in a tray— resolutions frozen in place by the euphoria of my temporary successes, the drive of my personality, and the emotional bruises left by the world. The process of waking up my faith was the gradual melting away of each facet, one by one, day after day of exposure to God's word and His Spirit, until intimacy with Him was born.

But this required an act of foolishness, where I rested instead of worked harder, sat down when common sense and tradition demanded that I stand, and reclined at Jesus' feet, like Mary, when my siblings in Christ suggested, like Martha, that I was misguided and lazy. It was a preposterous decision, but one that heightened my willingness to make even more decisions by faith, placing my complete trust in something that surpasses understanding, something illogical and often undesirable, and in spite of my feelings—known otherwise as "surrender."

By letting go and getting quiet, I learned to detect the sound of His Spirit, that still, small voice that dwells within mine and prompts it to listen and courageously follow His lead. Through this mechanism, He revealed to me that my soul must stop wrangling with my spirit and fall in line behind it. Rest was the first step, obedience by abdication, foolish resignation to be ruled by the sword of the word and led by the Spirit as the helping hand that wields it. This was a revelation I would desperately need to move forward, and to survive the next few months of 2010.

WILLINGNESS TESTED — READY OR NOT

By late summer, the miraculous income we'd received looked more like a mirage. Thanks to an unexpected expense, our resources were prematurely exhausted, forcing us once again into dire financial straits. Unexpected indeed was another choice we made by faith, my wife's faith in God and mine that she'd heard Him correctly — to begin homeschooling our girls immediately. With the added expense of curriculum and tutorial fees, the income calculated to last us through fall fell dramatically short.

So after two months of catching a breath in our new-old home, we had enough income left for approximately one final month — September 2010. Septembers are still quite warm in Tennessee, meaning it's still a good idea to have a well-serviced A/C unit — a duty I'd neglected as the homeowner and landlord who thought he might end up homeless, but one that I'd recently fought for as a tenant. Thanks for the reminder, God.

I'm not sure what I expected. The unit was ten years old and was literally held together on one end with duct tape. At a cost of just under ten thousand dollars, replacing it was impossible. Even the price of a service call would prevent us from covering my car payment. As our only reliable car, with just a handful of payments left, we were almost psychotically determined to avoid losing it.

Additionally, because of our credit history and struggles with the bank, we'd been warned that one missed payment would accelerate the foreclosure process. Right through the eye of the storm and into the other side we went. Although we'd been given approval to pay a reduced mortgage amount, we continued all summer to receive calls from different and apparently disconnected departments. One person gave us the nod to move forward; another kept asking for paperwork.

There were never-ending fax requests for hundreds of documents, the same documents every week, but for different reasons.

"Please fax the back of each page so we can see that it's blank."

"Please refax these twenty-nine pages and circle the numbers."

"Please keep trying, as the fax machine is busiest during work hours."

Check stubs, hardship letters, tax returns, income and employment questions were sent week after week until we had to start over each month because it was all out-of-date. Phone calls were a daily interruption — some helpful, others asking why we were paying less, and even those wanting to know if I was looking for work. To which I would say, "Well, actually, I'm living by faith today," knowing they'd think it was a joke.

The timing to teach our children at home couldn't have been worse, as other skeletons simultaneously jangle-jumped out of every closet to put the fear back into our fresher and apparently still fragile faith. September brought a barrage of legal letters and court summonses over year-old debts acquired early on as an attempt to keep everything afloat, debts I'd sheepishly ignored. Ultimately what looked like a better season for my family had suddenly become our worst. By the middle of the month, with an attorney standing by, we'd given ourselves a final week to consider bankruptcy as an option to remove the debts and just prayed that God would intervene.

FLINCHING BUT NOT FORGETTING

Once again, in spite of all I'd learned, my spirit fell flat on its face as the questions began to fly from every mouth, including my own. It was all true. I had no one to blame but myself. I was a guy who turned down a large salary to live by faith. With all the appearances along the way of being an idiot, this moment topped them all. I was indeed an idiot, a complete offense to anyone with a sound mind.

But in the midst of my defeat, the impressions of God's will became more vivid than ever to remind me, thankfully, that an immature seed remains dormant without the light of His Spirit, and that my spirit was fully prepared to take the lead. It was preparation that began to take root only weeks before, as Holly's revelation shed new light on our situation through a front porch conversation we'd long since forgotten.

After years spent pulling on heaven for answers impossible to discern through logic, desire, or emotion, I was learning to rest by refusing to listen to the part of me that had always been in control. My struggle was no longer a wrestling match between the parts of my soul, but one between my soul and the part of me that is spirit — the part of me created to detect and comprehend the mysteries of God as His Spirit reveals them. It is the same foolish notion that Mary had when she sat down instead of helping Martha and the same lesson Peter had to learn by allowing Jesus to wash his feet when it made no sense. By reminding me of the ministry dream I once had, God was challenging me to listen the right way — not the obvious way. The reward of meeting that challenge was a profound growth spurt, but one that required two years of suffering to activate and the coax of God's voice to inaugurate.

Ultimately, learning to rest is the first step in the program of surrender — the willingness to be the guest at Jesus' table instead of the waiter. Awareness comes not by hanging suspended in soulish contemplation, as I once considered, but by leaning on and pressing into God, searching for Him earnestly, not only through prayer and worship, but through the word.

When the word is approached intimately, expectantly, without all the normal agendas, it becomes the very instrument that recalibrates a man to be led by his spirit (the dwelling place of God's Spirit). The word fine-tunes a man's spirit that it may hear and be led by the voice of God's Spirit.

Until Holly's reminder, I was an adolescent spirit trapped by a middle-aged soul—a man still gazing through that blurry school bus window. That night brought the crescendo with a few simple words that I heard—"Wake up faith"—along with an overwhelming urge to write for Him to encourage and inspire others on His behalf, a ministry, if you will, that required no credentials or long-term means. It was during this brief period, about three weeks before our trials intensified, that I started my blog, "Wake Up My Faith."

MOVING FORWARD THROUGH THE WORD

I also began to study His word as if my eyes were naked and infant before it, my mind unleavened by opinion, as if every word were created just for me with the exactness and precision of all that He created. My heart grieved over the ideas I'd become familiar with as a believer, ideas that treat the word like a cheap costume with four red-letter, engraved gold buttons—like something we've outgrown and thrown to the side but kept the buttons as cherished heirlooms.

God inspired me to approach the word with absolute trust, to set aside the dirty spectacles of practicality and human wisdom—to knock with certainty as if it were the door that only His personality could answer. As a result, I began to discern the plagues of my past, relegating God's power to the past and a more hopeful future, and parading its characters and their creator as if only cartoons worth quoting in the present. I began to have disdain for the logical sneaks and theo-you-name-its who hive off chunks of the word into sentiments and stings, as if a deity who could speak entirely itself into existence might struggle to say exactly what He means.

Even by logic, a divided house falls — He either did it all or did nothing at all. Meaning every single word, whether in red ink or black, spoken by prophet, king, physician, fisherman, or a collector of taxes, whether from the mouth of Jesus or those inspired by His Spirit, is supernaturally intact. And the incredible journey of inspired people, technology, wars, motives, martyrs, monarchs, and the like have never been smart enough to throw His plan off track. It was either meant for the willing, whether rich or poor, simpleminded or genius, to be trusted completely or not at all. The more time I spent, the more He revealed, the more intimate our relationship became. The more intimate our relationship, the stronger His impressions became.

For me, His word became the floor of my wilderness, the ultimate place of rest and the door to the sound of His voice, the shepherd's hook to pull the sheep closer for a better listen. At one of my most pliable moments, battered from the perfect storm, with a moment to rest in the eye, God was revealing that resting in Him alone would be the only way to pass faithfully through to the other side. He wanted me to write about what I'd learned and continue to write as I learned. Interestingly, I'd been jotting prayers and journaling my thoughts for some time as a way of encouraging myself to remain faithful. But from this moment forward, these words were also meant for others. The decision to follow that impression at any cost changed my life for good. And serves as a living testimony that absolute faith in God is the only way to truly know who we truly are.

Journal Entry #20

Stowed for carry in a soul-shaped box with bright
     bands and hinges, but no key for the lock
In chasing the "what" we lose all sight of the "why"
     and bury it deeper the harder we try
We take it to work and coffee with friends, or lob it at
     wisdom, maybe she can break in
Buy oodles of books that prove and describe a biblical
     truth that still feels like a lie
Mining the minutes and days in between, we labor for
     contents that labor cannot glean
We've been given a cart that we think is a horse, a
     soul full of value with no direct course
Unless, of course, we are willing to see that soul-
     shaped boxes have faith-shaped locks and spirit-
     shaped keys
Soul-shaped box — my identity, my gifting, my
     potential, God's expression, His light for dark
     places
Faith-shaped lock — my willingness to rest, to listen,
     and then courageously to follow the instruction
Spirit-shaped key — God's intention, plans, and
     appointments, His specific will for my life

God's expression is tucked in a soul-shaped box that
only He can unlock. The box itself is His gift to me; what
He placed inside is His gift to the world around me. My job
is not to pry it open, but to carry it and all its potential by
faith as a flicker of light into the canyon of darkness — like
a clay pot percolating with light but one that can only be
cracked open when it collides with darkness. There is a
point in our suffering when we stop asking God to change
our circumstances and trust Him enough to rest perfectly

"in" them. Only then will the sun pass directly over the deep pit of our dark circumstance and reach all the way to the bottom — illuminating for the first time what our suffering has produced. Faith isn't about living each day as my last, but about living as if each day belongs to God, and remembering that not one person ever walked away from Jesus, unloved. Welcome to post-salvation life.

THE TANGO BETWEEN SOUL AND SPIRIT

When it came to trading our mortgage payments for home-schooling, I was excited by it, emboldened by the opportunity to step once again into absolute faith — the same kind of faith required to decline a high-paying job for something God described as "better." Unfortunately, I'd forgotten the part about it being "harder." As soon as the A/C unit crashed and a court summons arrived, I could almost see my kids grabbing what little cash we had and stuffing it in their backpacks on the way to homeschool. Woefully, I reconsidered how one missed house payment could send us packing, throwing us all out of our home and school. Like a military tank, my soul went back in gear and for a moment nearly crushed my spirit. Life got harder, and I panicked. God had just taught me an incredible lesson about the direction of my life, but I was already forgetting that He wasn't about to let me tiptoe down a side street to avoid the obstacles.

In a spasm of homespun initiative, I sent letters to creditors warning them to cease and desist, attempted to repair the A/C unit myself, and began a mad search for any kind of employment I could get — never realizing those letters are great for collection agencies but fruitless when the bank has an attorney on staff. Or that grappling with an A/C unit when your only qualification is bravery is as intelligent as playing leapfrog in the attic.

One second I was bear-hugging sheet metal, the next dangling frog-legged from the ceiling of the room below — our new convertible bathroom. But by hook or crook, from greasy spoons and grocery stores to bug patrol and lawn care, I'd find a paycheck somewhere with my name on it. It was panic perhaps, or a soulish slice of practical pie thrown into the eyes of my spirit — the very part of me ready for victory, but teetering on the sidelines, having tripped over a six-figure income to arrive at a minimum wage.

Steeped in win-the-battle-lose-the-war irony, I gladly accepted when a longtime friend offered part-time work at her pharmacy. It was kindness on her part really, and faith in my willingness to learn something I was unqualified to do. Orientation began in the break room as the sounds of clock punching, microwaving, and musical phones jumping trailed off with friendly glances from employees taking conversation-sized bites between rings — sensations unfamiliar to me, routines I hadn't known for twenty years. I'd forgotten them, I guess, while staring through the office window of a million-dollar home.

Having never set foot in the back room of a pharmacy, my expectations were simplistic, understatements cobbled together in a mental scrapbook of sore-throated visits. Reality, however, was quite different from pill counting in pastel smocks, a marvel of intricacy and exact sciences — sliding corridors of assorted miracles divided and waiting for just the right headache, hernia, or hacking cough. And worst of all were the prescription labels, with infinite combinations and potentially fatal consequences from a misprint.

I was mesmerized by the operating speed and acutely

important instructions, lost like a slowpoke in a speed puzzle contest where the loser goes to prison. Impressive, I suppose, overwhelming to say the least, and a multitask nightmare for a dad who struggles to order at a drive-through window. I wanted no part of this death by a thousand details, a task that was so incredibly opposite my personality.

Sometimes God allows our own subtle will to become a wilderness, not that we should beg, but that we would tire of laboring for answers and listen instead to the beat of His heart by simply resting against it. The truest test for a soul still learning to rest is facing and choosing between the obvious demand of circumstance and the less conspicuous demand of faith:

Finding a job when you have no money is a good idea.

Listening to God is a better idea.

The tango of common sense and the extravagance of foolishness that is either sustained with a soulish yelp — "Listen, you dope, finding a job when you have no money *is*, according to Scripture, listening to God: having to work to eat, etc." — or, on the other hand, is dismantled by the human spirit, indwelled by God's Spirit, which discerns the subtle difference between walking by faith and scrambling chaotically by sight.

THE REWARD OF FAITH IS ALWAYS BETTER

Taking on the fast-paced work of dispensing medication when you have the responsiveness of a mug-shot is a bad idea, no matter how desperate your obligation — and paradoxically, the best thing you could possibly do, if by the Spirit of God you were led to it. As my orientation day came to a close, it brought the relief of one final weekend to reconsider my decision, a weekend I chose to spend with God, not agonizing but listening.

Through the word, intimate meditation, and Fatherly rev-elation, His instructions were uncomfortably curt and clear. I would honor God by accepting the job, not out of common sense or because we needed the money, but simply because He made the unsettling offer and by faith alone I had to take it. So I made the decision, not by the demand of my soul, but by the lead of His Spirit through my own — a sliver of distinction that makes all the difference in who gets the glory. And in the end, this was the difference between becoming His expression and missing the mark entirely — exactly what I had been doing for twenty-five years.

Study, prayer, and meditation that particular weekend deliv-ered the wake-up-my-faith call needed to move me forward as a writer for Him, a download of His thoughts that would be confirmed in a matter of days, when what looked like a slice of idiot à la mode had the taste of manna from heaven on a supernatural platter. On the heels of a nudge, three weeks of intimate study, and one finely tuned final exam came the ulti-mate victory — a feast at Jesus' table by Holy Spirit invitation after twenty-five years of slumber in the comfort of my own understanding.

The following week's to-do list consisted of on-the-job train-ing and bankruptcy, just another twist in the road, we thought, until it twisted again at the very last second and confronted us head-on with the absolute last thing we expected. A series of things, in fact, as logic defying as a cartoon roadrunner in Scripture, who always ends up with a win.

By mail, we received an unsolicited check with the sugges-tion that we use it to pay off my car. The amount was three thousand dollars, exactly the right amount to make it ours for good and redirect those payments toward groceries.

Shortly after, our front porch welcomed unexpected an out-of-the-blue truckload of groceries and a Styrofoam cooler full of meats and casseroles—enough to last for several months, allowing us to trade grocery money for an overdue service call on the air unit.

By midweek, two A/C repairmen shared the bad news that we needed a new heating and cooling system, just as I had suspected. But the bad news came with a wink, as they had found a way to get it running and keep it that way for next to nothing. "It won't last long, but all is well for the moment."

And incredibly, at the end of the week, without the slightest inclination, I received a straight-outta-left-field request for eight weeks of my time, which included a paycheck with the promise of meeting our needs for the better part of the coming year—making it clear that God was giving us time to rest at His table, in His labor, and to share the good news with others.

Nothing like a week full of blessings, one of the best we ever had as a family. But as a family still limping about for another crippling reason, God hauled off and made it our best season. And the very best blessing of all was the call from our prodigal son that weekend, who was on his way home for the first time in nine months.

CHAPTER 13

JUST ENOUGH SAND

Journal Entry #21

In the face of harsh persecution, early Christians had a clever method of revealing their identity to one another while concealing it from those aiming to suppress the church at any cost. It's been said that first-time meetings began with a believer reaching to the ground covertly and pushing aside just enough sand to form a crescent-shaped line. If the other person was also a believer, the gesture would be quickly reciprocated to complete the fish symbol—the one most of us are familiar with today. If not reciprocated, the believer could identify the other person as a potential threat and remain quiet. But in the face of modern Christian culture, where faith is inadvertently superficial and grace is sentimentally ambiguous, just enough sand to draw a fish is not enough sand to draw a distinction.

A SAFE DISTANCE

"A woman with a child is one I'll never marry." So I said—until I did. I met my son-to-be when he was two, and I married his mom when he was three. Sometimes saying "never" is a good investment. Nevertheless, an instant family is unwillingly tethered to a bit of instant stress. And like any good investment there is risk of some regret—in spite of our promises.

Wedding day vow to my son:

"I love you, son, and always will, but God will always love you more. I promise to do my best as a father and friend, but even when I fail, I will be truthful with you. I promise above all to point you to the Lord Jesus as your Redeemer, King, and Truest Friend and to lead our family in His ways all the days of my life. I will always pray that by His strength your life will be lived for His glory."—January 1996

Loving my new son was easy, but I found that loving him from a distance was easier than standing in line behind him. So I chased my wife's heart directly while she chased after his well-being and we chased our tail in circles without ever blending a thing, certainly not a family. She'd been a prizefighter on his behalf, but to my surprise she'd never left the ring. And there was no single expectation, commitment, or concern tougher than being in her corner when I knew her back was turned. But it wasn't ringside applause she wanted or scriptural support from the corner. She wanted a husband who would jump in that ring and love her son like a father.

Sometimes when our burden seems heaviest, God adds a bag of sand. Not for tearing our heart at the seams, but to get our knees to bend. When I learned to bend down and love her son, my wife learned to stand up and love her husband. Truth is, we need more than just enough sand to draw a fish. We need enough to tip the scales.

Journal Entry #22

Indeed, God's plan is for spouses to hold one another above every other, including our own children. But His plans are built by patient hands for bruised and broken hearts. Rome wasn't built at the speed of an instant family, but any family built by God will not fall apart like Rome. Sometimes God's plan is a set of plans that take time to unfold gradually. And only gradually can we become each other's first priority by learning to begin as each other's last.

A DIRECT BLOW

Few pleasures intoxicate the soul of a parent as deeply as the sweetness of a child's heart. Like our heavenly Father, we find a more thrilling satisfaction in loving our children when they appreciate us. We spend decades gladly sowing their good soil for a chance to witness that single harvest known as adulthood. So it's a nauseating discovery at harvesttime to find that the source of our once-sweet intoxication is now the rotting character fermenting in the field.

My son, at eighteen, was in deep trouble — not with the laws of man, but with the seduction of man's opinion. He had learned to live life so dishonestly that hurting people seemed a reasonable price for gaining favor with fools. And as his parents, dishonor was our bitter inheritance. Included were the lies to us and about us, the assumptions he allowed others to believe, and the harsh judgments of the misinformed that resulted. But most distressing of all was not knowing the true depth of godly soil left in his character after all the years of planting and waiting for something good to grow.

When confronted he made no apology, responding only by summing up his indifference into one well-timed, remorseless stare. It was a direct blow to his once single mom and champion for not coming to his rescue—not this time. And he began to leave without considering that it was also a direct blow to my wife—a moment when my anger grew feet and followed him abruptly through the front door and into the street.

With only an inch between the fog of my angry words and his hollow eyes, I made a final announcement: "If you want to hate us, then hate us, but you will never again treat my wife this way. If this is how you choose to live, you'll have to do it elsewhere." And with no phone, money, car, or clothes—nothing but icy ground beneath his feet—he turned away as the temporary courage of teen bravado carried each reluctant footstep forward. We hoped that he'd spend only a few hours becoming closer friends with regret, but he was gone for the better part of a year.

LETTING GO BRAVELY

My wife looked at the door, fell to the floor, and gave the son she painfully delivered eighteen years earlier to another sub-freezing January night. "Lord, this is my son. Do with him what You must." It's along the seams of a mother's heart that we find the strength of her devotion. Not because the seam won't tear, but because it's where she's most willing to bend. She let go bravely, as her own bag of sand began to tip the scales to our favor. This went on in the midst of our financial meltdown, as God continued to strip away our self-reliance. We'd lost everything, and now everything included our son.

To add insult to injury, he found refuge with people who considered us abusive and would not respond to our humble appeals. They took him in without a word, and by default fostered his staying away. The details we'll leave with God, but the lesson He leaves for us and all who will listen. God knows the pain of betrayal very well but has never once been surprised by it. We, on the other hand, are nearly always surprised by it. In the end it makes the soul sick if we, like the alcoholic, continue to hold the nose, cover the eyes, and drink the lie. We have to take the risk that will keep our children focused on God—even if we are hated for it. After all, what earthly risk outweighs the benefit of following the One who cannot be surprised? Nine months later, the phone rang, and we knew that from somewhere, courageously huddled behind tears of regret, our young man was calling with a broken heart.

Sometimes God wrestles the heavy sacrifice from our arms in order to get them in the air. Other times He adds more weight to get us on the ground. Our son had been carrying his own bag of sand for all these months until, finally, God gave him another one.

"Mom, Dad," he said, his voice trembling slightly and surrounding us with a gentle integrity, "I'm so sorry for what I've done, for the pain I've caused you. I was wrong. Do you think you will ever be able to forgive me?" With tears all around, I responded, "We love you, son, and we forgive you. Don't worry anymore. It's all in the past."

TIPPING THE SCALES

Just enough sand to draw a fish is no longer enough to define, determine, or distinguish our faith. If it feels like God is adding weight when His burden is supposed to be light, then surely He's adding to our depth by giving us more sand—one bag at a time until we learn to bend. The extra weight will tip the scales and the extra depth will bring our precious seed to harvest. Our son, now twenty-one, is preparing for work in ministry. He's a devoted student of God's word who loves to encourage others for Jesus. He honors us so much more than we could have ever imagined. Glory to our God, for He is faithful.

Letter to my son:

For me, the day you were born came two years after the fact when I saw your tiny, handsome face in the picture frame on Mom's desk. I had no idea what God had planned for the three of us. You were the victory of a single mom, and she protected you like a heavyweight fighter because for a year or two the two of you were all each other had. Loving you was easy, Tyler. Learning to be a dad was not. I'm sorry it took so long.

I remember fondly in the first few years that every bedtime story meant building a new truck from scratch. I would ask you how it looked, and you would add detail after detail until you fell asleep. There must be a fleet of those trucks still parked in my memory. But if I looked stressed, you would stay awake, touch my face, and offer encouragement from that little voice—the one that could never quite make the "y" sound.

And how the room would almost shake with excitement at every birthday and Christmas. Never were parents more convinced that they had given their son the very thing he wanted. We were so encouraged by your sincere appreciation. But I also remember that Christmas morning when I actually yelled at you for coming downstairs too early. You were so excited, and I bruised your heart. I'm ashamed of that moment—and a thousand others like it. The truth is, I was impatient and harsh with you throughout your childhood, and my heart will always ache over it. Yet somehow you always managed to encourage me when I failed, and you never withheld forgiveness. For that I am eternally grateful.

Then there were all those baseball games. We watched with pride as you led your team and ran bases faster than anyone on the field. But we were never more proud than when you encouraged your teammates—especially the ones on the bench who needed it most. Or the time you came home from school two hours late without a word or phone call—Mom and I were furious. Only later did we find out you were in the school parking lot the entire time, sharing the gospel with a student who had bullied you for months. These are memories we will always cherish because they gave us a glimpse of who you really are.

And later still—one of my favorite moments was the time you and I got lost together on vacation and walked for miles without a clue where we were going. But neither of us cared because for that instant there was only you and me as we truly are—a picture of our future. Thank you for giving me that. And finally, I remember the bitterly cold night when you left home in anger, with no phone, no money, no car, and no clothes—nothing but the icy ground to keep you company. We hoped that you'd spend only a few hours away considering what you left, but instead you were gone for nearly a year, considering how we could let you.

Tyler, there's never been a more joyful note than the ring of that phone and the sound of your voice for the first time in nine months. And there was never a more joyful day than when you returned home shortly after with a willing heart. Humility truly is the giant that only looks small to small people. In your trial you became that giant, and for the first time I could see it. We rejoice at seeing God's promise unfold.

For most it takes many birthdays to begin looking back across them all with gratitude. But occasionally there's a rare exception when a young man begins to listen for God's voice, looks back briefly to see what He's done, and is thankful. You are one of those rare people who've chosen to see what God has done and, in turn, sees the trajectory of what He's doing. As I look back across my own years I see that I'm thankful as well—thankful for being allowed to witness a miracle as my only son becomes my brother. Tyler, you are a leader and a great encourager meant to offer hope to all who cross your path. Hold on to that with all you've got—it's all that will matter in the end.

Dad's back-pocket proverbs:

1. Be surrendered to God instead of committed.

2. Seek God not just above all things but instead of all things.

3. Get intimate with God, and you'll arrive at the sound of His voice.

4. Focus on how much God loves you, and your love for Him will grow from that.

5. Remember that God is the provider and you are His conduit.

6. Make sure others see the "Christ" instead of the "Christian."

7. Love your mom and never forget how much she loves you (me too).

"Father, we lift up our son that you would anoint him daily as the righteousness of God in Christ, transformed by the Hope of Glory living inside him. Let every day of his life be an honor to You and a blessing to those You lead across his path. Remind him of Your unfailing love as You refine his character, and let Your Spirit burn faithfully in his heart as You assign purpose to each of his days. We surrender him and commit his life to You now as a young man of God, a city on a hill through which Your light will forever pass. In Jesus' name we pray, Amen."

This is the letter from my son two years after he left, about fifteen months after his return and several months into a new chapter of his life at Narrow Gate Foundation, a ministry we support where young men discover the path to purpose.

Dad,

I feel it's necessary to write to you and say I am so proud to be your son and to call you my dad. I had the absolute privilege of reading your blog post about me and our redemption story. I think it was beautiful, and I gave it to some of the guys to read. Bill mentioned he had read an article on your blog about me, and I was surprised and asked for a copy, so he printed one yesterday and I've already reread it multiple times. It was such an amazing writing. I enjoyed it and am very grateful for the fact that you took the time to write that. I think our relationship is such an awesome story, and the redemption aspect of it is so inspiring.

I found that the Greek word for redemption is *apolutrosis*. It comes from the compounds *apo*, which means "off" or "away" and *lutron*, which means "something to loosen with." The word itself means "ransom in full—deliverance." I find the word very fitting for our relationship with our Savior and also our relationship today. God is using you, Dad, in such a powerful and impactful way. You're an encouragement to everyone who comes in contact with you and your words—me included. After reading the post and after months of pursuing an intimate relationship with our God, I've had the chance to see just a glimpse of His character through you. God is using you as a vessel to spread hope to the hopeless and to spread light and love to a dark world that is riddled with sin.

Never once did I see or hear you turn your back on God. That is a true definition of humility, sacrifice, and selflessness. You never lost your focus on God, and in turn you grew more faithful in Him and His ways. You said it was a miracle to see your only son become your brother, but I see a miracle far greater than that. His design for the good, yes, but also for the bad things you've gone through, that your faith made your son want more than anything to be like his dad. It wasn't anything you forced. It was the love and dedication you emitted from your soul that produced change in your son's life.

You are the person I look to now for godly wisdom and godly strength, because how could I not? You're my dad and I love you more than I think I even knew was possible. I appreciate you. I love you. I am proud to call you dad. Last name doesn't mean anything to me anymore. You are more of a dad to me than anyone on the face of this planet. You need to know in my heart you're my papa and I am your son—always and forever. Never again will I hurt you like I hurt you then. I'm realizing more and more every day how big of a redemption story we have. It gives me hope because of you allowing yourself to be used by God, and I'm no longer afraid. Nor will I ever be again. I love you, Dad, with everything I am.

Tyler

HARD PRESSED, BUT NOT CRUSHED

He left in anger, January 2010, as God was severely adjusting our way of life and preparing me to write. In a tiny plaid house with no room for superficial faith or ambiguous Christianity, letting go of a struggling son was the most heavyweight choice we could make, especially for my wife, who'd fought so hard to protect him our entire married life. Home is where the heart is, and sometimes it's a tiny house where the heart can be properly broken. We left a lifetime of baggage at the front door on the way in and left a relationship with our son by that same front door on the way out.

You can't climb out of a well when you're busy falling in, despite all the "pearls of wisdom" flicked casually from the rim. And by the time you've hit bottom, you're too banged up to try. That fall took two years for us, and nine months for our son. We crashed to the bottom with a facedown thud—broken but alive and a little more humble, thanks to a few extra bags of sand.

It was our own small version of "hard pressed on every side, but not crushed; perplexed, but not in despair; persecuted, but not abandoned; struck down, but not destroyed" (2 Corinthians 4:8–9). Not until September of that year, back in our new-old home, were we made whole as a family—nor was I prepared to be made whole as a man whom God could wholly use.

CHAPTER 14

OKAY, LIFE'S UNFAIR...
WHERE DO WE GO FROM
HERE?

LEARNING TO SHARE

Christmas 2010 brought an ugly year to a beautiful end. The restoration of our son and the home we so eagerly left were the undeserved blessings that transformed our worst year into one of our best. Our celebration included a lifelong friend, my old partner in four-wheeled, lawn-chair adventure. He was my brother-in-arms who navigated the country with me in a VW bus, a kindred presence that made it altogether better for us and a little less lonely for him. He rejoiced with us in our happy ending, and we grieved for him over losing his family in a very unhappy, unjust divorce.

Our camaraderie growing up created a magnetic field of

curiosity, a common ground where yes-men could be best friends, daring one another to ease the pain of rejection by sharing conquests. Such as flying to Dublin with enough cash for the tickets ... but not enough for a place to stay—just to see what would happen.

What did happen was a couple of Yanks with a couple of stouts ending up spread out like wet noodles at a Dublin airport bar, hoping that sleeping there wasn't illegal. Our hope was dashed in short order by the shiny badge of an Irish cop named Dexter, a middle-aged mind reader apparently, who was friendly enough but very direct: "Morning, lads. You fellas short of cash or shy of directions?"

Before the second or third worn-out word rolled out of my mouth, he interrupted. "Just tell me this, what're your plans and when might the two of you be leaving?"

It was all a little too pushy for me in the condition I was in, so I pushed back a bit harder. "Why do you care? Are we not allowed to sit here?"

His response was worse than either dumb Yank expected: "Okay, fellas, why don't you grab your bags and come with me." And that was that—the "see what happens part" after coming all the way to Dublin, short of cash and shy of directions, to figure out how to dodge an overly ambitious airport cop.

Already ten steps ahead, Dexter knew every inch of that place and waved us on, outpacing our ability to question. Like jet-lagged sheep to the slaughter we followed without a peep, until the half-minute sprint to the exit ended precisely where he planned. Heading for the door, I wondered if loitering at an airport was even possible. With an about-face and a few steps in reverse, he raised both hands and motioned us to get a move on. It occurred to me then that his aim was to throw us out the door literally, like a bouncer.

Sure enough, he lurched forward to one-hand grab each of our shirts at the shoulder. "Serendipity, boys," he said, shocking us both.

"Serendipity! Easy now, I've got room enough for the both of you and the wife's a real talent in the kitchen. My shift is over now, so if you're in, then off we go!"

We were in for three days of Irish hospitality. Mission accomplished.

And off we went directly into adulthood with new families, careers, and a little less curiosity, old friends indeed with cama- raderie forever attached to the hundreds of risks we took, and the highlight reel to prove it. But by middle age, that friend of mine was a man of God separated indefinitely from his growing family by a thousand miles and a giant cloud of ignorance. For the first time, that magnetic bond meant nothing, because there was nothing to say yes to, zero to laugh about, and nowhere crazy enough to go that would relieve his pain by leaving it behind.

Thrown for a loop over all the verses and clichés, I was confronted by friendship without a meaningful thing to say or knowing how one counts losing a family at Christmas as all joy. Reminiscing about the exploits of youth is a charming tradition, but one that matures quickly when the present is so utterly convincing. *At least he has my family*, I considered. But then again, so did I — which made his dilemma all the more painful to witness, when being a witness is all I had to give.

Three days of wee-hour conversations, with a gallon of coffee and tobacco-filled cups, drew out the poison — three decades of being convinced by living proof that life is unfair, yet long- ing to be, hoping to be, and even expecting to be treated with fairness. Two middle-aged men who'd done so much together as kids had learned only one thing as friends — not that life is sometimes unfair, but that fairness itself is simply a myth. Because no matter what our circumstances were, neither one of us got what we deserved. Maybe we love God best by sharing in His pain so we can love our neighbors by sharing in theirs, forgetting about what is fair.

EMPLOYED BY GOD

It was a new year with a new lease and the same plan, as another remnant of hope dropped directly from God's hand into ours to continue this journey of learning to live by faith. After settling a few debts and avoiding bankruptcy, we had just enough cash to last through the summer for the second year in a row. At least that was our hope. Thank God for the gift of work, truly unexpected work that was, as far as we were concerned, the signature of God.

For the second time in a year, we received calls that were impossible to grasp through the common sense of conventional wisdom — which I imagine was exactly the way God wanted it. Some considered it luck; others rationalized it as part of the framework of my earlier success in business, remnants of previous work or relationships still loosely available for emergencies. But I have to clarify that these instances arrived without notice, prior solicitation, or the slightest hint of more where that came from.

In fact, the projects were never intended to be contracted, especially to a guy in my incredibly unstable financial position, or one without a business. They were independent, miraculous moves of God, full-on demonstrations of His faithfulness.

Some saw it as a blessing of stopgap survival, God's way of keeping our bodies alive until we could get back to normal. But for us it was income from heaven that kept our faith alive so we might never be normal again.

As a result, it seemed evident that God was offering a continued season of rest, more time to develop our faith by actually having to live it out. Not so evident, however, was how He intended for me to use this additional time or where the wrong decision might lead. Aside from the steady flow of remaining debt issues and the maintenance of everyday life, my waking hours — according to most — should be spent seeking long-term provision.

Maybe redefining survival as God's faithfulness was the best evidence that my own faith had finally severed all ties with worldly ambition as well as common sense. I chose instead to seek the One who provides and to write about the journey it took me on — an idea that still offends the minds of many, considering the magnitude of our outstanding debts and foolishly unsecure future. What I didn't choose was the relationships that writing about God's faithfulness would bring — men, women, husbands and fathers, wives and mothers, precious souls who found something redeeming in the words our mutual Father had poured from my soul. Encouragement backed by living testimony that God indeed is a good Father, one whom we can trust with absolutely everything — literally.

Offering hope through His word and our testimony was the only agenda. It was not what I considered a ministry at first, just a great way to be used by God. But one that eventually required hours of actually spending time with individuals. To my surprise, the online community of believers was a spiritual mission field, overwhelmingly underserved with everyday people in need of hope. Not the flowery words from an adolescent writer, but real encouragement breathing with vulnerability and the fresh wounds of an ongoing testimony.

In a world of gurus in hot pursuit of stature and influence, Christians included, I was astonished to find that people of all ages were listening to a man who cared about nothing less, and nothing more, than to be honest about God's love, which requires suffering and throwing caution out with the Christianese bathwater. I had nothing to lose or gain by writing honestly about our struggle but the good pleasure of my Father, who presented the opportunity to do the better, harder thing.

The speed at which God increased the online connections was not at all what I expected, nor was it something I could ignore. He continued to place in my path all manner of believers weary from years of grind-it-out Christianity, good folks who desperately wanted to rest in God's arms but weren't quite sure how, what it looked like, or where to draw the line. The fact that we were still learning ourselves brought kinship, and being able to testify with living proof of God's goodness delivered the satisfaction of pure ministry I'd been longing for.

So my days during the first few months of 2011 were spent writing a little, encouraging a lot, and poring over the word in search of God's personality. I suppose it became my full-time job, employed by God, genuinely on His payroll. By choosing to seek God, not just above all things, but instead of all things—especially income and career—I learned to an even greater degree how to detect the sound of His voice and be consumed by obedience to it—my only means of movement, my only sense of direction.

Journal Entry #23

God was teaching me to minister to others and by spring had given me a proverbial laundry list of lessons, Post-it notes for the soul perhaps, reminders that His expression is so often obstructed by my own agenda.

- Authentic surrender severs all ties with ambition unless it glorifies God or loves another in His name.
- The God who cannot fail is the same one who lives in us. Victory is assured when we let Him lead.
- Suffering is friendship with God, the honor of the sharing in His pain that liberates us from the passing fancy of friendships with others based on anything less.
- We have so much to say, and yet none of it matters unless it elevates our precious Lord and triumphant Friend, Jesus.
- Christ is irresistible. Christians are not. It's Jesus' love that people crave, not my well-intentioned agenda.
- Blood relatives are important, but blood-bought relatives are eternal. We must love the family of God, as family.
- The sneaky difference between giving away something trivial and something costly is usually the attachment of our name.
- In regard to pointing out the sin of others, I have only two hands—one to point at my own sin and the other to point toward my Redeemer.
- In service to others, let us lower our expectations of people and raise them of God.
- Godly compassion covers the wounds but leaves the truth exposed.
- Never add a "but" to God's word, and always add a "but God" to man's word.

LEARNING TO RELY ON GOD'S ACCOUNTING

Surprises—we love and hate them, as they have such great potential to shift our mood or direction. One thing Holly and I never counted on was reaching the point of no longer being surprised by God's goodness or by the trials that allowed Him to display that goodness. In late spring, we received a foreclosure letter, a "special edition" notice that described our home as *already in* foreclosure, ten days from auction. This was a new kind of surprise, a more robust version with teeth that bit through nearly a year of on-time payments made faithfully as instructed. According to the same bank that offered us the lower payment, we were now in default and had been since the month we moved in. Pure genius!

After all the brawling over faulty information and rambling on about rights, the bottom line was a first round knockout win by one of the world's largest banks. We had nothing in writing, no proof that we'd ever been instructed to pay less—and to the victor go the spoils. The demand of our ambidextrous opponent was immediate satisfaction of the debt—the difference between our reduced payment and the original pre-modification payment, from the beginning. The amount was just under twelve thousand dollars, and we had ten days to pay—no ifs, ands, or buts.

By God's grace we had the money and by faith we paid it, not simply to save our home and not out of fear, but because it was clear that this event was one that God had already accounted for months earlier. I'm not suggesting we were dancing for joy that, once again, our financial plan was thrown off-kilter. But the truth of God's goodness, the idea that we could rest in our Father's arms like children had become tangible, touchable, and, surprisingly, reliable—even in the face of ridiculously unfair situations.

My reliability, however, as a man proclaiming the virtues of walking by faith, continued to be tested and proven hypocritical. As the days grew warmer, those vivid revelations of spring began to dissipate and fade behind the subtle pride of suffering with success. Rest took on the posture of hollow boasts that wavered with each dollar we spent and every groan from the attic, a sound that returned with a vengeance as our decrepit A/C unit was nearing death and screaming to be put out of its misery.

No matter how many times God provides, by tiny gradations we forget through the eyes of the soul, as if the mind, will, and emotions are stamped with evaporating ink. The characters of Scripture were equally vulnerable, but the great blessing of the indwelled spirit is that through it God continues to write new chapters until we learn to discern directly from the source. Memories fade, but God's Spirit remains.

BECOMING THE VILLAGE MONSTER

One step forward, half a step back through the conditioned response of practical thinking. God had provided for our basic needs, which certainly didn't include replacing a ten thousand dollar heating and cooling system, an expense that, even if we paid by installment, would throw us immediately back to the wolves. Nevertheless, the unit, as predicted by the professionals, was only a few degrees from permanent overexertion.

The atmosphere was one of cool mornings spent pretending that afternoon temperatures might not rise, and midday cringing when it did. The noise was horrific. Yet within a few days of its opening swan song, about 4:00 p.m. on a Wednesday, we heard an even louder noise just outside on the east side of our house.

A breathtaking miscalculation by a young neighbor severed

the natural gas line beneath our living room, and within minutes our home was so flammable that answering the phone could have killed us. But because of a self-appointed deadline, our gas line was easier to break than my concentration. My wife stopped explaining and pulled me by the shirtsleeve away from my desk and through the front door. Our A/C unit had been wrestled to the ground by a black SUV and hogtied with the other end of that gas line. I dashed back inside to turn off the breaker and open windows, but it was too late. My game face—the one that looks like Jesus—was dead on the floor from asphyxiation. Seconds later, I was back outside, this time glaring at the wreckage as if it were a prison break with every guard asleep.

If sixteen years in the passenger seat is considered "driver training," then the SUV sitting atop our air unit wasn't there by accident. Our neighbor's son (the untrained driver) blew out his sixteenth candle, garnered a license, and nearly blew up our home. His maiden voyage to the soccer field gave way to a circus maneuver that went no farther than the side of our house. The fire department arrived in full hazmat regalia, unleashing a parade of armchair crisis managers into the street. Neighbors love this sort of thing.

The young man's father turned to me as I approached, and with a humorous expectation he crossed his arms and said, "Well, neighbor, it's time to get yourself a new unit."

But humor is an unfamiliar idiot when your house is about to explode (and you're broke). My wife and I were equally frustrated, but she was more overwhelmed by the opportunity to "be Jesus" to our neighbor. I just wanted to stripe the poor fellow with Jesus' bullwhip—you know, the one from the temple? And I made it quite clear.

To my neighbor's defense rushed another neighbor from another street, making her way to my yard in hopes of inspiring the villagers, still other neighbors, to grab their torches and pitchforks—me being the monster. There were loud chants of "oh, grow up" and "come on, it was just an accident." But after the kid destroyed our air unit, wiped out the utilities, and nearly killed us, ridicule for not laughing it off in the first two minutes was a marked improvement on the hour.

FROM UNFAIR TO DOWNRIGHT CRIMINAL

We expected the neighbor's insurance adjuster the next business day. Seven days and seven estimates later, he knocked on our door with camera in hand. While shaking my hand, he was shaking his head in disbelief over the condition of our unit. "I've never seen anything like it," he said. Scrolling through the images, he continued shaking his head. "I can't wait to show these to the other adjusters." I humored him, hoping the bottom line wouldn't take as long to reach as his arrival. With a nod of agreement, he stopped abruptly and blurted, "You'll need to call your homeowner's insurance."

"Call *our* homeowner's insurance?" If you're reading between the lines, look for a large deductible and a rate increase in that proposition.

"Sorry, sir, it's just our policy."

My wife, the woman who'd been ready to be Jesus to our neighbor, was now ready to drive out this thief with that bullwhip—the one I'd stolen from Jesus. I think he escaped unharmed, but with a ten thousand dollar replacement cost, we had no choice but to agree to the hefty deductible and to live with higher rates. By this time our sense of fair expectation was roadkill left for dead on the pity highway.

Our own adjuster arrived three days later with an expert, a partnering A/C company to help validate the process. We had already had seven experts assess the damage and agree on the solution, but certainly didn't mind one more. By now we knew that federal law prohibited partially updating an obsolete system. Our safety and legal compliance required a full replacement, and hearing that for the eighth time made little difference to us. Or so we thought.

To our surprise, this final expert hinted that all seven of our estimates were fraudulent, suggesting that rebuilding was actually a better option because it would reduce the claim cost by half. Even though our system was ten years obsolete, matching parts could be located in junkyards. Wow, how wonderfully convenient for them. And how awkwardly disastrous for us when they sat down at our dining room table and waited confidently, with our adjuster, as if it were an offer we couldn't refuse. Unfair began to feel downright criminal, and we both broke out the bullwhips. Thankfully, despite their stirring advice, we did have a choice between them and the lowest price of the other seven, and by God's grace, the entire unit could be replaced for the cost of our deductible. Unfortunately, we'd have to give up our next house payment to do it.

So let me sum this up: My wife and children are in homeschool and I'm working in my office. Our neighbor, who's not quite ready to drive, demolishes our gas line and A/C unit. We narrowly escape our gas-filled house without blowing it up. A few people are condemning me for lacking a sense of humor. The damages amount to just under ten thousand dollars, and we have no A/C, heat, or hot water for weeks. The neighbor's insurance refuses to pay for it, and our own homeowner's insurance has a one thousand dollar deductible. Our monthly rates increase by 15 percent, and our insurance preemptively offers enough to rebuild it with junkyard parts. And in conclusion, the kid next door who injured only his pride was now zipping past the mess he created, with more confidence, in his brand-new car!

YOU SLICE THE CAKE — I'LL PICK THE PIECE

"Okay, life's unfair ... where do we go from here? And where does the notion of fairness come from anyway?" On the one hand, we admonish one another to leave our enthusiasm for fairness at the door — "Sorry, life just isn't fair." On the other, we charge one another to procure it ambitiously at all costs. It's a conundrum I'd been wrestling with for months that was all too easy to blame on Jesus. But after this kind of test, one that could have killed my family, that kind of lightweight simplicity was begging for heavier clothing.

Surely Jesus wasn't teaching us to be hypocritical, yet we advise one another as if He might be okay with it at the appropriate time. His standard for loving others is simple enough: "Treat people the same way you want them to treat you" (Matthew 7:12 NASB). But if we're not careful with the application of that verse, our flesh gravitates subconsciously toward the best "me" outcome, twisting the emphasis so that later, under pressure, we're relying on a false expectation: *People will also treat me the way they would like to be treated.* And we behave according to something slightly off-parallel, which eventually shuttles our thinking in the opposite direction.

Without fail, every person we shared this story with had

some version of the same response and remedy: "The neighbor should pay or help pay our deductible." I certainly agree that it's the fair thing to do. But if I ask myself why, every honest answer leads me to the same perplexing place, and it's not Jesus. The bottom line is, Jesus doesn't teach us to be fair. He teaches us to love even our enemy—to be more than fair to everyone, expecting nothing from them in return, which effectively makes the concept of fairness for a Christian, whether giving or receiving, irrelevant.

Perhaps our neighbor *should* pay or at least help with the deductible. Or perhaps he *should* say, "Well, you're getting a new system for a thousand bucks. I did you a favor." And he'd be right. But none of it matters if my complete trust is in God. Holly and I prayed sincerely about this dilemma and waited for God to give us instructions—instructions that ultimately included nothing about fairness or compensation. In following His lead, we sat down with the young man, alongside his parents, and let him know that it was okay, that we'd both made much worse mistakes as teens and that all was forgiven. And considering my behavior, I asked His parents to forgive me for my anger. We left without saying a word about compensation but trusting God to be our provider in yet another impossible situation. One week later, the neighbor brought us a check that covered the cost of our deductible.

I suppose if I were a journalist, I'd have to say my assignment for the season was learning to let my light shine a little more—but making doubly sure it's always pointed at the cross, especially in the midst of inequity. One of the most startling revelations, still difficult to distinguish, is the unrelenting difference between the concept of fairness and the God who lives beyond it. Fairness is a sweet idea, but if we make it our god, it makes the hope of grace a lie and our faith as conniving as a thief. God's love, whether given to us or expressed through us, has a much sweeter taste than "You slice the cake and I'll decide which piece."

In spite of all the rich blessings we'd received to that point in 2011, facing another fall season with an empty bank account and no income would prove to be just as challenging as the last. But our resolve to continue this journey of relying strictly on God, knowing that a plan was unfolding, kept us from blinking for a little while.

PART 4

A FOOL'S REWARD ...
AN EXTRAVAGANT GOD

CHAPTER 15

MASHED POTATO

WRITE FOR ME AND I WILL PROVIDE

Relying on God is a message preached from every pulpit; relying "strictly" on God is not. Popular faith requires little more than a nod, while authentic faith requires a willingness to suffer. Unfortunately, the call to take up our cross is a message whose only champions are those faithful few with splintered hands. But if the God of the Bible is real and really not a politician, we're left with one legitimate choice, because only authentic faith reveals the fingerprints of God, and suffering prepares our character for leaving them on the world.

By midsummer we were broke once again, but not quite broken enough to understand that only an empty hand can open the door of opportunity—and broke is a tiring way of life when all one sees is the empty hand of God and not the cross we've been given by it that our own hands won't touch. At least we were brave enough to pray for provision by asking instead for His best intention, and by interruption, decree, or an unrestrained rebuttal, God answered my prayer right smack in the middle with what I call "a note from the King." It was a revelation so paralyzing and distinct that for me it became our pivotal moment of absolute clarity. The burden, however, of having to trust that your spouse has truly heard from God might mean following them into chaos while considering whether or not it's an over-the-top act of insanity.

My note from the King, written exactly the way I heard it:

"You've been searching the skies for a cloudburst while standing in a pool of water—you don't have to talk Me into providing for you. Instead, embrace the depth of this struggle and steward it well. My water is gathered and stored here in your lowest place. Stop asking for rain and plant the seeds that I've already given you. And from the rich wet soil beneath your feet will spring trees of living sacrifices among the weeds. With a renewed mind I have given you this wilderness to civilize. With the light of men I have given you this darkness to illuminate. With my leaven I've given you this fire to make everything you touch rise with you. And having crushed you like salt, it's with My hand that I will scatter you and make savory the culture that surrounds you. Write for Me and I will provide."

Inspiring, indeed, from His mouth to my ear, yet so lofty a notion that merely reading aloud in solitude inspired my own doubts—self-doubt, that is—of the snot-nose, little-ole-me variety. But His plan is not one that requires self-confidence or sideline support, but only supreme confidence in the face of all opposition. According to all that I'd witnessed, authentic faith—faith that is moving and pointed in God's direction—will always be afforded the fuel to keep it from ever stalling. And once again, through a twist of irony, we received exactly what we needed, a rebate check from the same mortgage company that had recently demanded one from us. Evidently, by short selling the homeless landlord house, we'd been enrolled in an incentive program that provides an allowance for "moving out." Nothing like a dose of God's reality to perk things up—and one that kept our mortgage current for the next two months.

Still unaware that writing was anything more than a way to encourage people, I continued to follow what I believed were His instructions, trusting Him for provision, yes, but motivated by passion to please Him. Writing for Him gratified the only ambition left in me, yet somehow remained an unselfish labor. So despite any lingering doubts about my abilities or "it won't support a family" apprehensions by my wife, I chose to listen only to Him. Several weeks after the rebate check arrived, I was greeted by an email message that another work project, similar to the last, would be initiated by September, and for the first time my services were included in the budget. Fantastic news indeed, as it would settle our differences momentarily, and it served as further confirmation of my personal decision to simply "write for Him."

A FOOL FOR A SPOUSE

With God's provision, the lesson for summer 2011 was obvious: What God is saying is always the right answer, so it's much more efficient to develop our listening skills than self-confidence or common sense. Not so obvious was an equally important revelation that would unfold thunderously over the next few months as the income promised by September failed to materialize. Through that struggle God began to reveal His purpose for our lives, and learning the extent of that purpose demanded the kind of testing that would either make or break our marriage. Moving forward wasn't an option until every germinating seed of discord was yanked out by the root. We had to become more than two sets of gifts trespassing through individual mission fields. God wanted us to be as one before Him, not just in marital duties, but in faith as a solitary unit for the encouragement of others—something not possible when caution becomes a disease.

October delivered all the proof a weary wife needed to rightfully say, "My husband has lost his mind." Who would blame her? I was like a hobbled acrobat vainly refusing to dismount, and she had a fool for a spouse, a man still unwilling to budge when not a nickel or a gallon of milk could be found in our house. With the promise of income by September suspended in silence and a status that guaranteed foreclosure with a single delinquent payment, in her mind it was "time to face reality." Not taking action meant more than losing a house; it meant that our children might be without a home for Christmas. Additionally, our commercial bank chose this moment to sue me as guarantor for the enormous debt of my now-defunct business.

Even gray-haired faith, the kind that ages gracefully with every courageous act, can seem meaningless when the weary bodies attached are so mentally, physically, and emotionally flat. That note from the King was nice, but simply not enough to overcome the sheer exhaustion of our up-and-down-only-a fool-would-try-it lifestyle. She'd had enough, but at least there was boldness in her decision to face reality. I stayed the course but wavered about like an absolute failure in our disagreement.

DID YOU SAY POTATO?

The mind-bending difficulty of having to choose to believe and be obedient to God instead of trying to rescue my family or comfort my wife resulted in the worst, most detestably nauseating few days of my life. One of those days was Halloween, when both of us, visibly depressed, were invited by an acquaintance of Holly's for chili, a backyard fire, and hopefully a bit of encouragement. The husband of her friend, a man I'd never met, began by asking me a perfectly normal question.

"Keith ... it is Keith? So tell us a little bit about yourself, like what it is that you do for a living or what you might like to do if given the opportunity. You know, your dream job—what does that look like?"

In fear I mumbled the answer, hoping he wouldn't actually hear it. But he did, sort of.

"Come again. You what? You want to become a mashed potato?" Surely he was kidding, I thought, so I didn't respond until he asked it again.

Finally I said, "No ... not a mashed potato; I'd like to become another Max Lucado."

The hard part for me is that he didn't laugh until I said "Max Lucado." Of course, the misunderstanding made for an easy chuckle, but the loftiness of my newfound ambition is what drove home the negligible bit of sarcasm.

Maybe he was right. It's all right to dream but anyone stupid enough to gamble his family for it has to be a fool, or at the very least a genuine potato who was indeed about to be mashed.

My spirit was hanging on for dear life.

THE BLESSING OF EMPTY HANDS

Journal Entry #24 — November 2011

Hope deferred makes the heart sick, but hope without faith pulls the plug and watches the heart die. The fall season has now arrived as an empty-handed messenger. The income we'd hoped to see remains the income we hope to see eventually. Until then, we've stopped paying our mortgage in order to cover essentials. Better to face foreclosure in the next few months than to face the next few weeks without food and utilities. In the hands of another messenger, perhaps our own version of Goliath, came a six-figure lawsuit filed recently against me, now set in motion. It's a long story about rights — the rights of a bank to pay an attorney to convince a judge that a man with nothing can pay back everything from that nothing. With an income that appears to be lost on the horizon, I cannot defend, I cannot replace, and I cannot outswim this tidal wave born from the aftershock of my failure — a failure that continues to break my heart for the sake of my family.

Never before had the holiday season seemed so trivial, but meant so much. So dimly lit were these days that by November hope deferred had indeed become hope unplugged. And so we did stop paying our mortgage in order to cover essentials, but the weeks evaporated like inch-deep water in the heat of our circumstance, leaving us nothing but tears — tears I buried in the pillows of my couch. There I sat with my beautiful wife beside me like an angry passenger. She'd been watching patiently for months, watching me do nothing with my days but pray and attempt to write when our children were already decking the halls of a home they were bound to lose. Write when a lawsuit was ushered to our door by an armed official, and write when there was little food left in the pantry and no way to buy more.

"Kevin, I can't live like this—we can't live like this—it's insane!" That empty-handed messenger had us both by the seat of the pants, but we were moving in opposite directions.

"Write for Me and I will provide." The words God planted in my spirit were not a secret, but they were no match for the voice of her reason. I looked at her as she looked at the empty pantry, choking on the utter foolishness of those words. Still, they hung in my gut like poison.

"I can't explain it, Holly. I just know that I have to do this."

She was in tears, not because we were suffering, but because she was carrying a much bigger burden—the burden of having to trust that a man like me had truly heard from God, which is easier said than done when her children are asking why that pantry is so empty. It's the moment of truth when spouses grab their children and run for safety. I deserved nothing less.

The hours passed slowly. My words and prayers stuck to the floor. There was nothing I could do—nothing but wait and wonder aloud if God is indeed still generous, and wonder silently what a generous God might do with such an extravagant fool. And like any fool on the worst day of his life, I gave up. But like any truly faithful wife with a fool for a husband, she did not. She didn't leave, because by faith she had the courage to make a different choice—to lift my head and boldly say,

"Kevin, I'm terrified . . . but I am always with you. I'm with you no matter what."

Within an hour, barely long enough for our tears to dry, I received a note from a new friend: "I have a surprise for you. My editor is interested in your story, and I'd like to introduce the two of you. Can we talk?" Forty-eight hours later, a door swung open without a single knock or push from my hand. Behind it were the carefully placed words of that editor, filled with kindness and backed by authority. But of those words, the ones that stood on the shoulders of all the others were these: "Kevin, write me a book."

That same afternoon I received yet another call, this one from the client who still needed help with a large project, one held hostage for two additional months by budget constraints. Not only had it been approved, but it came with an offer to pay a portion of my fee in advance. That's right—two big doors opened by two big empty hands in a single day. Halleluiah! The work took several months to complete and left no time for writing. But by the spring of 2012, God had provided enough income for me to pursue the other opportunity full-time—to write for Him so others could be encouraged by our story.

I suppose that when God's hands appear to be empty, it is because they aren't meant to carry a thing. Instead they're meant to open the doors of opportunity and then applaud the infant steps of faith that carried us to them.

CHAPTER 16

ONLY WHEN GOD BECOMES ALL THAT WE WANT

UPSIDE DOWN

Funny, I never considered myself a writer until God stood my faith on its head and shook out all the common sense—a perpetual requirement, apparently, for all who desire to walk upright in an upside-down kingdom. By January, with a publishing door open and every need covered for months, writing as a mission was the only thing I could imagine and, suspiciously, the only thing that made sense.

It is impossible to please God without some measure of faith, but the prospect of living life entirely by it is viewed by most as impractical, unnecessary, and even foolish. After being encouraged by a world-class publisher to write a book, completely unsolicited, I was more convinced than ever that becoming an absolute fool was the only goal worth having. After the book was rejected by that same publisher and several others like it, I realized that I'd finally achieved that goal in the most extravagant fashion.

From the hope of encouraging many to an unemployed clown sent packing by a rodeo for better writers, I had nothing to show for this God-given opportunity but the heckles and horns of statements such as, "We didn't fall in love with this one." "Too much of a downer." "Didn't seem to have a point." "Sorry."

So after several years learning to live by faith, I remained unconvinced as to which is more foolish—being willing to do anything for the Lord or being willing to believe He would do anything for me. It's a question God would eventually answer in the most dangerous place for a man full of zeal and no common sense—a very large church, in session, filled to capacity.

A FORK IN THE EYE

Sunday morning at ten fifteen the words "stand up and sing" formed in the air and lingered there like those of an unforgettable friend. And ten minutes before the sermon was supposed to end, I heard them again and again. "Stand up and sing . . . sing 'Jesus Loves Me'!"

I looked around at a thousand quiet souls and wondered who it might have been. Some were craning toward the pulpit to catch every corporate word, while others had their arms outstretched and were nodding agreeably at what they'd already heard. But no one, including the speaker, had requested a song or singer to interrupt what is decent with something completely absurd . . . like "Stand up, Kevin, and sing 'Jesus Loves Me.'"

I looked at my watch, then down at my feet, until clarity

wrapped around my dignity and began to sink its teeth. Either God had a plan and had taken time to speak, or I was about to be crowned church idiot and king of all freaks. If God indeed has a plan, then He surely has a voice, but sometimes He just hauls off and forces us to make a choice, knowing full well that a quick fork in the eye is always better than a lifetime of staring at one in the road. So my moment of truth came down to this: Avoid the entire charade and risk offending God's Spirit, or move forward obediently and risk offending the minds of men. With legs a-prickling and every ounce of blood attempting an escape through my face, I two-handed the back of the chair in front of me and began pulling myself into place — a standing position. And inching into my periphery was the nauseating blur of faces who were about to be embarrassed ... for me.

Journal Entry #25

Faith comes by the hearing of God's word, but only with rigorous testing will its measure increase. To that end, any David willing to dance before God with all his might must first count the cost of being despised by others in exchange for his Father's delight. If we consider ourselves to be sheep in the fold of Jesus — those who hear His voice and follow — then the question arises: What would we do if He asked us to raise our hands and worship Him on the front porch or in the supermarket? Or maybe while in the mall or jogging with our iPod? The question is not whether we think it's unnecessary or even senseless, but instead whether we know the sound of His voice and are consumed by obedience to it.

MAKING BRICKS (WITHOUT STRAW)

Continuing to think of myself as a writer was an act of obe-dience, but considering myself an author, especially one with such a cheery testimony, seemed more like an act of glory-to-me self-indulgence—and for good reason, according to those who know best what readers care about. I suppose if I'd had a day job, this would be the right time to tend to it and move on. Thankfully I didn't, and even more thankful was I for the God-appointed friendship that developed with the editor who first encouraged me. Although she wasn't able to single-handedly publish my work, she never stopped believing that our meeting had a deeper significance or reminding me to trust that God would eventually reveal it. "Don't give up, my friend. God has called you to do this."

She was right. God had indeed opened an impossible door—but by this point it looked embarrassingly like He'd done it for the guy in line behind me. Letting go of a book intended for someone else to write was my cynical delight, and "the faster the better" was better than just all right.

On the other hand, being denied the opportunity to encour-age more than a few people—people like me with their own set of cheery circumstances—was heartbreaking. While the income already provided would sustain us for months to come, certainly long enough for me to sit down and write a book, wasting it by groveling for second chances from publishers would only make things worse.

Sometimes God presents an opportunity and provides the means to carry it out, but then He turns our faith on its head by making us wait to move forward until neither the opportunity nor the means are left—kind of a "make our bricks without straw" moment that breaks the back of logic by forcing us to face what we truly believe. So I held on to the challenge of my editor friend, despite the advice of those who know best to worry less about writing such unpleasant things and to curl up instead with a happier, snappier type of faith already written on the walls of the Christian hall of fame.

Rather than moving on to a "more prudent" use of my time, I chose to use our season of brief stability to pursue the skill of writing, leaving its future and the welfare of my family with the One who makes bricks without straw and books without having to withdraw His intention. Some call that foolishness — we call it faith, a life of learning to live by the sound of God's voice, which simply can't be comprehended by a head full of common sense. (Special thanks to Noah for building that ark.)

By late summer, we'd been awarded yet another substantial work contract, which seemed to confirm my decision by holding out the promise of meeting our financial needs for the year ahead. But as the project began with great hope, so it began with a series of hopelessly unexpected interruptions. Like some cosmic instant replay of the year before, three months and twice as many postponements later, our summer of great expectation had given way to another November of desperation.

Hoping I will not waste what Jesus did for me on wanting anything more than Him is, I suppose, the sentiment of a lunatic. After all, without the benefit of this income we'd lose every inch of ground that was gained the entire previous year, and more. But lunatic or not, we hadn't forgotten that throughout this journey the Lord, without fail, had sustained our every need by His abundant provision. And all the more generous at times, He has grown our faith by withholding that provision until all seemed lost. So once again, with Christmas only weeks away, a delinquent mortgage and every resource exhausted, we waited patiently for the good news to come, until finally—with no time to spare—it came. We rejoiced that the project delays were over—*Hallelujah!* On the other hand, the project was also over, cut from the budget at the eleventh hour without warning.

Obviously, I'm not a pastor, theologian, or teacher. I don't have a church, a fan club, or a flock. I'm just a regular guy with a testimony who would rather tear away empty pockets than fill them with empty promises. Before any of us can stand on the banks of the Red Sea and believe that its waters will be parted, we've got to learn the sound of God's voice, like Moses at the burning bush, and then be consumed by obedience to it, in spite of the doubting opinions of others, like the children of Israel, who would rather remain comfortably in bondage. The call of suffering isn't a beastly request by God that we moan on the floor for His sake, but instead it's the willingness to deny oneself and follow absolutely nothing in this life but Him. It's the willingness to be foolish in the hope that we won't waste what He's done for us by wanting anything more than Him— which might be as simple as standing up to sing when others will not.

JESUS LOVES ME

By now, I was halfheartedly standing in church, like the lone, awkward applauder at a social event or the guy who tried and failed to start the wave in a stadium, about to become the gladiatorial fool who disrupted the entire service to stand up and sing "Jesus Loves Me" ... loudly. With a brief glance at the auditorium door to weigh my last options for avoiding embarrassment (I could have easily made a dash for the bathroom), the other half of my heart joined rank against my flesh and laid itself on the altar.

Just as the hymn whispered up from my spirit, the words "do not offend the speaker" settled on my shoulders like the insisting hands of a remarkably strong grandfather. My posture recognized the escape long before my understanding and slumped without hesitation into a deep sigh of thanksgiving. *Praise the Lord!*

Then, with only a minute left in the service, the speaker led the congregation in prayer before making a strange request: "You know what, folks? This is going to seem cheesy, but before we dismiss, let's all stand up and sing 'Jesus Loves Me.'" And without hesitation I knew! I knew that the Lord had just restored what the thief of my struggle had stolen. Jesus loves me — He really, really does.

Three days later I shared my experience with the pastor. After a momentary pause, he looked at me with conviction and said, "Wow, Kevin. It wasn't until the closing prayer that God gave me that song for the congregation. It wasn't planned or even thought of until I prayed." We both smiled and pondered the love of a God who reminds us He's there by testing the limits of our willingness. And I knew for sure that a God who would captivate me audibly and confirm it is a God who would never allow the needs of my family to go unmet or ever forget His plans for our future.

LOGIC, LUCK ... OR FAITH — PICK ONE

The process of living by faith is a gamble, one that only a man sick of relying on the world is willing to take, especially in the aftermath of a broken promise — that simple surprise that typifies the retractable slither of corporate words to little guys with the emotion of a five-word text: "Sorry, no budget. Happy holidays." *Thank You, Lord, for a logic-wearied soul that freed my spirit to listen to the extravagantly foolish things on Your mind. But honestly, I'd much rather write for You and trust that You'll provide than stand up and sing solo before thousands who have no idea why.*

The good news arrived shortly after the bad in the form of an offer to write my story (warts and all) by a publisher willing to give it a try. "Write for Me and I will provide." God had spoken to my spirit. I did and He has. "And while you're at it," He said, "cast all your cares on Me and I will sustain you." We did and He has by giving me representation from one of the world's foremost Christian literary agencies and a home with one of the largest faith-based publishers—not an easy thing for an unknown, especially a contrary goof with nothing to offer but a dose of living proof that God is much kinder than our Christian behavior implies.

He has also taken care of our every need for more than four long years despite the jeers of brighter minds, as preparation for such a time as this—a moment when the rare privilege of pointing to Him exclusively and His credit for the victory are both undeniable under any form of scrutiny. And though some may disagree with our theology, not a soul on earth can explain it away by logic or call it all luck.

The timing of the gamble, on the other hand, is ours alone to decide. *"I've got something much better for you if you're willing to choose Me instead—though it will be hard."* Being asked to write a book by a publisher of this caliber was the opportunity of a lifetime and clearly the "better" thing God promised several years earlier. Having to do it in three months when I was flat broke would of course be the "hard" part of that promise.

While the advance was generous by any standard for a first-time author—half up front, half when the manuscript is complete—we could rely on it to cover only about one-third of our already frugal living expenses, not including our mortgage. As a novice with maybe ten pages of a book, a legally bound deadline, and no way to pay the mortgage, I had a potentially life-changing decision to make: spend every waking hour writing, even on the neighbor's lawn should we lose our home—a distinct possibility—or go back to a more "common sense" way of life and make a desperate attempt to find work during those hours.

Honestly, having our last resource stripped away at the eleventh hour had worn us down to the point that we simply had no taste or patience for the superficial. We were sick of putting more faith in a light switch to light a room than in a God we knew intimately to light our path as the lamp to our feet. He was either a cartoon in the sky or living by faith is the only way to know who we really are—any of us. Our decision should be obvious by now and serve as proof that the more we are willing to courageously trust Him with our life, the more willing He is to trust us with His plan. And in this we rejoice: " 'What no eye has seen, what no ear has heard, and what no human mind has conceived'—the things God has prepared for those who love him" (1 Corinthians 2:9).

SANCTIFIED EFFORT

For the record, undertaking such an adventure was not without effort. Holly is a wife, mother of three, homeschool teacher, paid aerobics instructor, and church volunteer, and—after bending God's ear—she was given the additional role of accounting assistant with a company made up of people who love her like family. Truthfully, she championed the idea of me writing a book more faithfully than I did under the circumstances.

We were both well aware that a publishing contract was a gift from God. But my approach to stewarding such an implausible task called for wisdom I simply didn't have. Thankfully she did. *"Lord, let it be Your delight to show Kevin how to write under the intense pressure of our situation, and if it pleases You, provide for me another way to help."* Her petition was immediately met with a part-time position that fell effortlessly into her lap.

The impressive thing is that she wasn't motivated by fear, a reasonable response for a spouse in her position. Instead she was led by the hand of God to labor at His discretion. The extra income was not nearly enough to meet our financial needs, but it gave her a meaningful way to help that didn't interrupt her other God-appointed responsibilities. So my wife is amazing, not only for giving a heroic effort, but because she listens to God and understands the difference between worldly and sanctified effort.

Some of our favorite objections by "Christians":

"Homeschooling is noble, but now's the time to forget nobility and get yourself a full-time job."

"Yes ... but these days everyone's a writer—your real job is to put beans on the table."

"Sorry, helping a man who won't get off his butt will just keep him coming back for more."

"Sure, God is good, but we live here, in reality. It's just plain selfish to put anything above your family."

Laughter after the pain was natural, I guess, as sharp stings begin to hurt less and even tickle a little with thicker skin. Compassion, on the other hand, was a struggle, undermined perhaps by a covert pride that God eventually uses the foolish things to confound the wise. Or maybe just my frustration over the enigma that attempting a life of faith meant somehow that I'd lost all God-made ambition, curiosity, and desire for approval. But I was and remain the same spirited personality who achieved financial success, gave at least 20 percent of it away, and enjoyed the comforts of a million-dollar home.

God hadn't forfeited my soul to heighten my spirit. He simply harnessed it to His through a season of temporary suffering, a condition designed by love to make walking by faith a lifestyle. So goes the challenge for a man who stands on his head in a right-side-up world where faith is viewed as a lack of ambition, wisdom is the fear of everything but the Lord, and fools get the chance to write books about it.

IMPOSSIBILITY BENDS TO ITS KNEES

Someone recently asked my youngest daughter what kind of work her dad does. After giving it some thought, she said, "Well ... he types words on his computer—and then deletes them." Which is exactly how I would describe it if I had her integrity. Thank you, daughter, for reminding me that faith is an irrational process, one that appears on the surface to be nothing less than a fruitless pass from one haphazard mess to another. After thirty-five cans of tobacco, five bags of coffee, two bottles of Tylenol, and another handful of miracles, something emerged from all that typing and deleting that challenges me to keep digging a little deeper.

And hopefully to remember that the beginning of faith is not a mere passing from one mess to another but a sequence of events designed to teach us that we are less than we thought—less than our onetime accomplishments, less than our courageous steps, and even less than the wisdom we think we've gained. But God is more than we hope, more than we believe, and always more than we can see. As we become less than we think, He becomes more than we can imagine; as we become weak, we receive the ultimate strength and begin to accomplish impossible things. Let not only the content of this book but also the fact there is a book stand as a living testimony.

It was written in the first half of 2013, a period when there simply was not enough income to stay in our home, maintain health insurance, or completely pay our utility bills. It was the worst possible time to plant myself in front of a computer and attempt to write our story—and the best possible time for God alone to receive the glory. And to Him alone it goes.

That handful of miracles included two random checks from our mortgage company paid on behalf of a class action suit over unfair foreclosure practices. Additionally, we received several donations from friends who share the belief that struggling believers might be encouraged by our journey. And finally, God has opened a new door and offered us the opportunity to develop a new kind of ministry, one that teaches by example how to rest completely in the Father's arms like happy children.

GOD DOES EVERYTHING BRILLIANTLY

The reward of walking completely by faith is what Christians long for but so many are unwilling to risk everything for, because it forces us to dethrone good things such as our marriage, children, identity, and career and replace them with Jesus as the true King. The stakes are just too high and the outward difference is subtle enough to rationalize. So we go on striving for God's affection and missing His intention—His desire—to fully express Himself through each one of us while we're here. God used the struggle set before my eyes in 2008 to remove a thousand from my soul by 2013, saving my marriage and my life, giving me children who are on fire for Him, compassion for the weary, and a purpose-driven life, lived out. As I see it, absolute freedom bought by the blood of our King is wasted if we refuse to become absolute fools for such an extravagant thing.

Journal Entry #26

The willingness to believe in the foolish things:

In an upside-down kingdom, it's the foolish things, not the practical, that glorify the King. When the fool has a need, he meets the needs of another. When his hands are empty, he offers his hands instead. When his storehouse overflows, he remembers that life is a vapor and counts giving a much greater privilege than making his future a little safer. When he is maligned, he is kind, and when he is about to faint from depression, he offers high praise to the Lord and for others he makes petition. When he's counted by men as foolish in faith, lazy when things look tough, and lucky when things seem great, he rejoices, gives thanks, and reflects on these onetime foolish things:

God made a way for Noah to escape, Sarah to conceive, Isaac to leave the altar and Abraham to father nations, Jacob to prosper over Laban, Joseph to feed the nations, Moses to deliver a nation, Joshua to win the Promised Land, Gideon's three hundred to prevail over more than a hundred thousand. And God gave David the favor for an everlasting throne, Elijah the speed to outrun a chariot and power to feed a widow for months from a single meal, Jeremiah the zeal to stand alone, Daniel the conviction to pray out loud and face death, Esther the favor at just the right hour, Nehemiah the vision to rebuild, and ultimately

He made a way for the birth, sacrifice, and resurrection of our Lord, Savior, and King of everything to exchange Himself for a bride.

If the prospect of living entirely by faith (in the One crucified entirely for us) is academically risky, impractical, and even foolish ... then our fork in the road is clear:

To one side, these bold men and women of Scripture are like wonderful cartoon characters we quote on occasion for practical wisdom. To the other, they are real people with blood-and-gut testimonies that have become the victories of our inheritance.

To one side, we see a savior pointing to our bootstraps who is willing to help if we're willing to grab them first. To the other, we see that only momentary affliction is able to burn away such a Christian-centered veneer.

To one side, we see that practical wisdom aims to make life safe by storing up treasure for later and avoiding risky mistakes. To the other, we see that wise decisions are not even possible when made by the spirit of fear.

To one side, we see the more sensible answers from the minds of men. To the other, we see the truth as it rings sincere through the veil of Christianese.

Only when God becomes all that we want do we truly see that He is all we need.

My hope for this story is only that it be compelling, real-life evidence that God can be trusted with everything—that He really is that good. For all who are tired of relying, even a little, on something other than God, today you can rest in His arms like a happy child. But if you need more proof, just come along with us to see what happens next.

ACKNOWLEDGMENTS

My special thanks to Holly, my wife, and to our three children. To a small handful of faithful friends who had the courage to walk with us through this journey, and to John Sloan for his skill as an editor and his unwavering dedication to providing the best possible experience for the reader. God bless you all.